HUMOR AMONG THE MINORS

HUMOR AMONG THE MINORS

TRUE TALES FROM THE BASEBALL BRUSH

Edward Michael Ashenbach

Edited by Jack Ryder
Foreword by Kevin D. McCann

BRAYBREE
VINTAGE EDITION

BRAYBREE
Publishing

This 2013 Edition published by
BrayBree Publishing Company LLC
P.O. Box 1204
Dickson, Tennessee 37056-1204
Visit our website at www.braybreepublishing.com

Originally published in 1911

BrayBree Vintage Edition of *Humor Among the Minors:
True Tales from the Baseball Brush*
Copyright © 2013 BrayBree Publishing Company LLC
King of the Minor Leagues copyright © 2013 Kevin D. McCann

No part of this book may be reproduced, stored in or introduced into a retrieval system or transmitted in any form by any means (electronic, mechanical, photocopying, recording, or otherwise) without the prior written permission of the copyright owner.

ISBN-13: 978-1-940127-06-4
FIRST EDITION 2013
Printed in the United States of America

About the
BrayBree Vintage Edition series

Many works in the public domain are available online in print and e-book versions. However most are of inferior quality, printed with generic covers irrelevant to the subject matter and little effort made to give the reader a clean, presentable book.

Each book in the BrayBree Vintage Edition series has a unique cover design relative to the subject. The pages from the original edition are reproduced in their entirety, with spelling and grammatical errors left intact. Printing errors such as faint type and missing letters and words are seemlessly corrected. Spots, blemishes, and stray marks on the original pages are cleaned. Each book includes an original foreword or other supplemental material.

This title was chosen for the BrayBree Vintage Edition series based on its significance to the history of baseball.

CONTENTS

Foreword—King of the Minor Leagues *by Kevin D. McCann*	xiii
Introduction *by Jack Ryder*	3
Career of a Cincinnati Boy.	5
Branches Out as a Mogul.	9
A Persistent Hustler.	11
The National Association.	13
What the Player Signs.	24
Outlawry.	28
Browning's Last Can.	35
A Trio of Stars.	36
Killed the Goose that Laid the Golden Egg.	41
A Lengthy Argument.	42
Riding Out on a Rail.	44
Dear Old Dixie.	49
A Bonehead Play.	52
Caught with the Goods.	52
A Quartette of Stars.	53
Coaching from Extremes.	56
Flirtation with Dame Fortune.	58
A Phenomenal Catcher.	61

An Exciting Series.	63
Humpty Badel.	65
A Stitch in Time.	67
Good or Bad Club?	68
Home Runs to Order.	69
A Cruel Deception.	70
The Bonehead.	73
Some Boneheaded Plays.	76
Retribution.	78
Let 'Em Alone.	79
Penurious Players.	80
A Plea for Sunday Ball.	82
Buying a Youngster.	84
A Sturdy Veteran.	86
Ramsey's Mustache.	88
Lost.	90
Sullivan's Clever Ways.	92
Homer.	95
A Pair of Night Riders.	96
The "Jerries."	96
A Somnambulistic Player.	97
Quite a Managerial Record.	99
Did Not Need a Third Baseman.	100
A Large Crowd.	101
A Queer Weakness.	103
Queen City Graduates.	106
Queen City Moguls.	110
Pals.	111
A Looking Glass Scrap.	112
Two Hustlers.	113
A Grand Record.	115

A Marriage on the Diamond.	119
Groundkeeper a Contract Jumper.	120
A Narrow Escape from a Fine.	122
Utility Players.	123
A Baseball Scout's Report.	125
A Slugging Match.	126
The Grandstand Comedian.	126
Nick Altrock.	128
A Two-Club League: A Sharp Trick.	131
Could Mike O'Conner Hit?	133
Hard Luck.	134
Worse Luck.	135
No Hair.	135
The Umpire Never Wrong.	136
The Crab.	137
Some Comedian.	142
Superstitions.	143
An Indian Story.	144
An Alias That Did Not Last Long.	145
Peculiar Playing Fields.	146
Dear Old O'irland.	149
A Bad Actor.	150
Arguments with Kelly.	152
Corcoran's Quick Wit.	153
Heredity.	154
Too Anxious.	154
A Kind Heart.	155
German Rooters.	156
Poetic Coaching.	157
The Sport of Kings.	158
Cy's Tip.	159

Observations in the Dining Room.	160
A Hold-Up.	164
John McGraw.	165
Connie Mack.	167
Hughey Jennings.	169
Before They Were Big Leaguers.	171
Dont's For Young Players.	171
Dont's For the Baseball Fans.	174
Managing a Baseball Team.	176
To A Young Leaguer. "Do Not Give Up."	178
Mileage Tables.	179
Index.	219

ILLUSTRATIONS

Edward Michael Ashenback	*Frontispiece*
Jack Ryder	iv
August Herrmann	12
John E. Bruce	16
M.H. Sexton	32
John H. Farrell	48
James O'Rourke	64
Two Philadelphia Pilgrims (Hoban and Graham)	80
Ashenback's Record-Breaking Team	96
Charles F. Carpenter	112
John McGraw	128
Connie Mack	144
Hughey Jennings	160
William Hart	164
William J. Clymer	172
Charley Schaefer	176

KING OF THE MINOR LEAGUES

EDDIE ASHENBACH was described as a "cheery, unconquerable optimist" who was "one of the most picturesque characters known to the game."[1] He was involved in practically every aspect for over 20 years—amateur and professional player, coach, manager, club owner, and league organizer. He was called the "king of the minor leagues" because he had spent time in almost every one of them. He was a storyteller who amused teammates and sportswriters with anecdotes about unusual plays, quirky players, and other aspects of life in the minors. As a player, he was regarded more for his defense and his colorful personality than his hitting. As a coach, he taunted opposing pitchers and entertained fans with his clownish on-field antics. Regardless, he was considered an astute judge of talent and tried unsuccessfully to add two Hall of Fame pitchers to the roster of his hometown Cincinnati Reds.

Born in Cincinnati, Ohio on October 18, 1871, Edward Michael Ashenbach[2] was the youngest child of German immigrants Joseph and Mariana (Franke) Ashenbach. He learned the game of baseball on the sandlots of Cincinnati playing for amateur teams

1. "News Items Gathered from All Quarters," *Sporting Life*, January 27, 1912, 17.
2. His surname was often spelled Ashenbach, Ashenback, or Aschenback. He signed his marriage license as Aschenbach. Hamilton County, Ohio Marriage Records Volume 124, page 382.

HUMOR AMONG THE MINORS

such as the Millcreek Bottoms, Bond Hill, and the Manhattans.[3]

At eighteen, eager to sign with a professional club, Ashenbach became a fixture at the offices of the local newspaper hoping for news of teams seeking players. He credited sportswriter Ben Mulford, Jr. with helping him get a tryout with the Canton Nadjys in the Tri-State League in 1890. He made the team's Opening Day roster and batted .190 in seven games played in the outfield and shortstop before his release in mid May.[4] Returning home, he told Mulford about one of his teammates, a hard throwing right-handed pitcher named Denton True (Cy) Young.[5] Mulford relayed his recommendation to readers of the *Sporting Life*:

> Ed Ashenback says that Young, of the Cantons, is a corking pitcher. He declares that it is a wonder he was retained at all, for there were over a score of youngsters under contract or waiting to be tried. He was signed as a catcher and put at once into the field. He caught two innings during his whole career as a Cantonian. Eddie's

---

3. Edward Ashenback, *Humor Among the Minors: True Tales from the Baseball Brush*, 6.

4. As early as May 13, Ben Mulford, Jr. reported the release of several Cincinnati area players from major and minor league rosters. "The executioner's basket is full of Cincinnati heads this week," he wrote. "Canton's management cut off Eddie Ashenback and Will Irwin at one fell swoop." *The Sporting Life*, May 17, 1890, 9. Yet in *Humor Among the Minors*, 37, Ashenbach claimed, "Our league [the Tri-State League] disbanded early in August, and I went back to the lots in my native town."

5. *Sporting Life*, May 24, 1890, 10. Ashenbach claimed in *Humor Among the Minors*, 37, that he first mentioned the pitching prowess of Cy Young at Canton to Mulford upon his return at the end of the Tri-State League's season in early August. This seems to be a lapse of memory on Ashenbach's part, as he had been released as early as May 13 (see footnote 2).

KING OF THE MINOR LEAGUES

ideas of the worth of the manager are not very exalted.[6]

But the rival Cleveland Spiders beat the Reds to Young, paying the Canton club $300 for his contract on July 30. Cy Young went on to win 511 major-league games and have a Hall of Fame career.

After sitting out the next season employed at a Cincinnati hardware factory, Ashenbach resumed his baseball career with the Harrisburg Ponies of the Class B Pennsylvania State League in 1892. When the team disbanded on July 14, he signed with the Allentown Colts in the same league. He split time between the outfield and shortstop, batting .195 in 58 games for both clubs. He returned to Canton, Ohio in 1893 as a pitcher and first baseman for the Deubers in the Ohio-Michigan League. He lost both games that he pitched and had a .267 average in 15 at-bats in a season shortened when the team disbanded on June 22.[7]

Before leaving for spring training, Ashenbach married Lydia Westermeir in Cincinnati on March 25, 1894.[8] Like him, "Lillie" was of German ancestry. He started the season in the Class B Southern League as center fielder for the Atlanta Crackers. A correspondent for the *Sporting Life* noted that "while

---

6. The first mention of Cy Young in *The Sporting Life* was actually made by a correspondent named Fielding published on May 3. He wrote: "Canton's new pitcher, Young, has been dubbed the 'cyclone.' He has wonderful speed and has splendid control over the ball. His future work will be critically watched by his many admirers." *Ibid* May 3, 1890, 12.

7. Ashenbach's statistics cited throughout this article were provided by minor league researcher Ray Nemec. Standings were taken from Lloyd Johnson and Miles Wolff, editors, *Encyclopedia of Minor League Baseball* (Third Edition). Durham, NC: Baseball America, 2007.

8. Hamilton County, Ohio Marriage Records Volume 124, page 382.

HUMOR AMONG THE MINORS

weak with the stick [he] makes up for it by his marvelous fielding, some of his one-handed catches while on a dead run bordering on the phenomenal." But his weak .203 average in 33 games eventually led to his release. He finished the season with three clubs in the Pennsylvania State League—Altoona, Reading, and Shenandoah—and batted .257 collectively for them.

When it came time to receive his final salary payment, the beleaguered Shenandoah management could only give him six dollars of the $35 owed him, which was not enough for a train ticket back to Cincinnati. Teammate Jimmy Toman "passed the hat" among the players to make up the difference. When another teammate felt guilty that he had money left over after his own ticket had been bought, Ashenbach told him, "Never mind, 'Weik,' hold on to your ticket, trust in God and remember Shenandoah."[9]

In 1895, former Atlanta manager Ted Sullivan recruited Ashenbach to join his new team, the Dallas Steers, in the Texas-Southern League. With Dallas, he had the best batting performance of his career to that point, hitting .313 with career highs in runs scored (106) and home runs (6) in 115 games. He also enjoyed the reward of playing for a pennant-winning club as the Steers (88-33) finished ahead of the second-place Fort Worth Panthers by five-and-a-half games.

During one tense contest at Abilene, where almost every spectator was armed with a revolver (even the umpire), Ashenback was playing center field as the Steers held a two-run lead. With the tying runs on base and two outs in the bottom of the ninth, Abilene's best hitter sent a towering fly ball to center. As Ashenbach gauged it, a fan shouted, "Boys of the Panhandle, to the rescue!" and some 5,000 revolvers were

---

9. "Topics of the Times," *Shenandoah* (PA) *Evening Herald*, October 9, 1894, 1.

fired at the descending ball. Through the smoke, bits and pieces of yarn fell at his feet and the tying and winning runs scored to end the game.[10]

His second season with Dallas in 1896 wasn't near as successful. He returned East to finish the year with the third-place Paterson (New Jersey) Silk Weavers of the Class A Atlantic League.

Ashenbach returned to the Lone Star State as an outfielder for the Fort Worth Colts in the Texas Association in 1897. By late June, however, he had reportedly "left that club in a huff and gone to Cincinnati." After a stint with the Houston Buffaloes in the same league,[11] he finished the season with the Springfield (Ohio) Governors in the Class B Inter-State League, where he batted .289 (second-best on the club) in 67 games.[12]

During the winter meeting of league officials, Springfield traded him to the New Castle (Pennsylvania) Quakers for catcher William J. Graffius on January 30, 1898.[13] There he enjoyed the best overall season of his 17-year playing career. He batted .281 with career highs of 31 doubles and 10 triples in 149 games for the fourth-place Quakers. Before the 1899 season, one writer reported that Ashenbach "did not enjoy good health" despite his success at the plate and "is now at Hot Springs [Arkansas] recuperating, from where he has written that he is in first-class condition." Unfortunately he got off to a slow start, hitting

10. Ted Sullivan, *Humorous Stories of the Ball Field* (Chicago: M. A. Donahue & Company, 1903), 213, transcribed in Jeff Sackmann, "Ted Sullivan, Humorous Stories of the Ball Field," *The Summer of Jeff* (blog), August 8, 2011, http://summerofjeff.wordpress.com/2011/08/08/ted-sullivan-humorous-stories-of-the-ball-field/

11. Ashenbach may also have played for the Dallas Defenders, also in the Texas Association, after leaving Fort Worth. *Sporting Life*, May 29, 1897. 4.

12. "Condensed Dispatches," *Sporting Life*, July 3, 1897, 4.

13. *Sporting Life*, January 22, 1898, 2.

only .197 in 29 games, and was released along with a pitcher in early June "to reduce expenses."[14] He finished the season with the last-place Schenectady Electricians of the Class C New York State League, batting .303 in 54 games.

One New York League writer in 1899 believed, "The only thing that will keep him out of the major League is weak hitting, as he is very fast as a fielder." But realistically, Ashenbach was 28 years old and his chances at a major-league career had diminished. Instead he explored other opportunities to stay in the game. He began a new phase of his professional career in 1900 when he became the owner and player-manager of the Hampton (Virginia) Crabs in the Class D Virginia League.[15] Despite player defections and a financial crisis alleviated by a public subscription campaign, the team finished in third place with a 29-29 record, 14 games behind the league-leading Norfolk Phenoms. Ashenbach himself finished the Virginia League campaign as center fielder for Norfolk, making his debut in a doubleheader against Portsmouth on August 25.[16]

As he did ten years earlier with Cy Young, Ashenbach tried to steer his hometown Cincinnati Reds toward another talented right-handed pitcher. Nineteen-year-old "Matthews" won 18 games for Norfolk and had tossed his first professional no-hitter against Ashenbach's club on June 12, winning 1-0. But once again, Cincinnati lost out and Norfolk sold the contract of "Matthews"—who was actually future

---

14. *Sporting Life*, March 4, 1899, 5; June 10, 1899, 10.
15. *Sporting Life*, February 3, 1900, 2.
16. "Hampton," Norfolk *Virginia-Pilot*, June 12, 1900, 8. "Hampton's Close Shave," *Ibid*, June 19, 1900, 11. Ashenbach's debut with Norfolk was reported in *Ibid*, August 26, 1900, 16.

KING OF THE MINOR LEAGUES

Hall of Famer Christy Mathewson—to the New York Giants.[17]

As Ashenback transitioned into the role of a playing manager, he exhibited a comedic style in the coach's box likened to such colorful personalities as Arlie Latham and Hughey Jennings. He entertained the fans as he jockeyed players on the opposing team and tried rattling their pitcher with remarks such as "the plate is moving." At Richmond, Virginia in 1909, he taunted club president W. B. Bradley so much that he left the game early. Often he was the only source of entertainment in otherwise uneventful or one-sided contests. "He is unquestionably the noisiest individual that we of the sporting department have encountered recently, and this is saying a lot," wrote one sportswriter about a game between Charleston and Atlanta in 1904. "What Eddie would say next soon became of more importance to the crowd than the game itself... He even talked a while on his fingers." Another remarked that he "looks like a good natured alderman on the coaching line, although he can make a noise like a Fourth of July celebration." Others thought he should join a minstrel show or perform in vaudeville.[18]

Ashenback returned as owner and player-manager of the Newport News-Hampton Shipbuilders in the revamped Virginia-North Carolina League in 1901. During the winter, he worked to strengthen the league and helped bring North Carolina clubs at Raleigh and

---

17. Ashenback, *Humor Among the Minors*, 40. *Richmond Dispatch*, June 13, 1900, 6.

18. *Sporting Life*, February 3, 1900, 2. *Newport News* (VA) *Daily Press*, March 23, 1910, 3. "Tri-State Leaguers Go Down Before Colts," *Richmond Times Dispatch*, April 17, 1909, 5. "'Noisy' Eddie Made Fine Fun," *Atlanta Constitution*, April 16, 1904, 9. "American Association Affairs," *Sporting Life*, June 15, 1907, 18. "Blinker's Observations," *Shenandoah* (PA) *Evening Herald*, September 15, 1894, 1. *Sporting Life*, November 26, 1910, 8.

Wilmington into the fold.[19] While his club enjoyed success on the field with a second-place showing in the pennant race by mid June, it struggled with low attendance figures due to a strike by shipyard workers.[20] On June 21, Ashenbach moved his franchise to Tarboro, North Carolina while the Portsmouth, Virginia club was transferred to Charlotte, North Carolina. The relocated Tarboro club finished the second-half of the season in second place in what had become a four-team league after the two remaining Virginia clubs dropped out.[21]

Afterward, Ashenbach went to the West Coast and finished the 1901 season as a first baseman, outfielder, and team captain for the Sacramento Senators in the independent California League.[22] Future major-leaguer Nick Altock recalled that when Ashenbach became upset at the players, he would fine them five or ten dollars. Altrock pitched for the Los Angeles Giants in a game against Sacramento and had walked eight batters but picked all but one off first base. Each time, Ashenbach said to the runner, "That will cost you five." When Ashenbach himself came to the plate and walked, he told the pitcher, "Here is one guy you won't get." Altrock challenged him to take his lead off the bag and quickly snapped a throw over to get him

---

19. *Sporting Life*, December 29, 1900, 1; January 5, 1901, 5; March 2, 1901, 9.

20. *Richmond Dispatch*, June 20, 1901, 3.

21. *The Sporting News*, June 22, 1901, 6; June 29, 1901, 5. *Sporting Life*, June 29, 1901, 17. With the departure of the two remaining Virginia clubs, the organization's name was changed to the North Carolina League. The final standings were published in *The Sporting News*, August 24, 1901, 2.

22. "Pretty Pennant Race," *The Sporting News*, August 24, 1901, 7. As William "Brick" Devereaux managed the Sacramento club, it is believed Ashenbach acted as team captain on the field with the authority to levy fines.

out. Ashenbach got up and angrily told his players, "Boys, the fines are off."[23]

During the winter of 1901–1902, Ashenbach was sued for divorce by his wife Lillie and had allegedly violated "an injunction not to molest his wife pending the proceedings." Apparently, there was a reconciliation at some point because they were still married at the time of his death in 1912.[24]

Ashenbach began the 1902 season as the coach of the University of North Carolina baseball team before returning to the professional ranks as player-manager for the Charlotte Hornets.[25] He guided the Hornets to a dominating first-half finish in the North Carolina League with a 39-8 (and one tie) record. From May 10 to June 11, they won 25 consecutive games to set a record for organized baseball at the time. "Their success lies very materially in the brilliant management of Ashenback," wrote one local sportswriter. "He knows how to get work out of the boys and his team work is magnificent." The Chattanooga Lookouts of the Southern League reportedly tried to purchase the contracts of practically the entire club (including Ashenbach) in late June.[26]

Among the players on the Hornets roster was a first-year medical school student from the University of North Carolina named Archibald Graham. Ashenbach had been his baseball coach at UNC and believed he was "the fastest man he ever saw in a baseball uniform." Graham would become better known by

23. Nick Altock, "Nabbing 'Em Off First," *Toledo News-Bee*, January 27, 1922, 15.

24. "News and Gossip," *Sporting Life*, January 25, 1902, 3.

25. Richmond *Dispatch*, February 12, 1902, 3. Richmond *Times*, February 19, 1902, 5. *Ibid*, March 11, 1902, 8. Ashenbach also coached at the University of South Carolina in 1909. "Base Ball Notes," *Washington* (D.C.) *Evening Star*, February 15, 1909, 9.

26. *Sporting Life*, July 5, 1902, 6.

the nickname "Moonlight" and immortalized in the motion picture *Field of Dreams*.[27]

Charlotte's success came at the financial expense of the rest of the league. When the last-place Wilmington Sailors folded on July 9, Ashenbach refused to play the second-half in a reduced four-club circuit. The league itself disbanded six days later.[28] He found another player-manager position that summer with the second-division Shreveport Giants in the higher classification Southern League.[29]

The Nashua, New Hampshire club in the Class B New England League recruited Ashenbach to be their player-manager in 1903. He had guided the team into third place and only four games behind the league-leading Manchester, New Hampshire club when he resigned on August 26 to accept an offer from the Evansville (Indiana) River Rats to finish the season as its manager.[30] He could do little in the final three weeks of the season, however, to improve the club's fifth-place standing in the Class B Central League. As a player, he was injured on the bases shortly after his arrival, though he hit .324 in 12 games.[31]

After helping organize the South Atlantic League in 1904, Ashenbach shifted into the role of team owner and president when he acquired the Charleston, South

---

27. Brett Friedlander and Robert Reising, *Chasing Moonlight: The True Story of* Field of Dreams' *Doc Graham*. Winston-Salem, NC: John F. Blair Publisher, 2009, 27, 30–31. *Sporting Life*, March 11, 1905, 3.

28. *Sporting Life*, July 5, 1902, 6; July 19, 1902, 1. *The Sporting News*, July 5, 1902, 6; July 19, 1902, 5. Ashenbach lamented, "The feat broke up my little league." Ashenback, *Humor Among the Minors*, 43.

29. *The Sporting News*, August 9, 1902, 8.

30. Ashenbach was suspended for ten games and fined $10 for an argument with league umpire Quinn on July 1. "South Atlantic Scraps," *Sporting Life*, July 16, 1904, 21.

31. *Nashua Daily Telegraph*, August 26, 1903, 7.

Carolina franchise. In addition to his responsibilites as manager, he also had to worry about selling advertising and tickets to finance the team as well as maintaining the ballpark and playing field. "I was now a full-fledged magnate," he recalled in his book *Humor Among the Minors*. "[A] venture that was backed by nothing but a little nerve and hard, consistent work bid fair to prove a large success."[32] He fielded a competitive team and finished the season in third place, six-and-a-half games behind the inaugural champion Macon Highlanders.

On August 24, Ashenbach allegedly spiked a young boy following a loss in Macon, Georgia which led to a search for his whereabouts by a mob and the police. He recounted the incident in his book seven years later. Ashenbach, still in uniform, was on a crowded streetcar and felt someone reach into his hip pocket where he had put his club's share of the gate receipts earlier. He grabbed hold of a young boy's hand and as he struggled to free himself, Ashenback unintentionally stepped on the boy's foot with his spikes. Not knowing of his attempted thievery but believing Ashenbach had done it on purpose, the crowd became a mob and chased him to the team's hotel. The Macon manager and a kind woman helped him escape and get to the police station, where the truth was revealed and Ashenbach was exonerated.[33]

An article published at the time contradicted this version of events. It claimed that local fans were teasing him on the streetcar about his team's loss and that Ashenbach "was insulting and profane in his talk, notwithstanding the fact that there were several ladies on the car." The manager kicked the boy, who then "hit Ashenback in the head with a block of

32. Ashenback, *Humor Among the Minors*, 59.
33. *Ibid*, 46–49.

wood." Once he stepped off the streetcar at his hotel, he allegedly spiked the same boy as well as another one. "This was too much for the crowd," it was reported, "and a mob at once made a rush for the unpopular manager." Evidently Ashenbach was arrested, as a "prominent gentleman" from Macon posted his bond. He claimed the boy tried to steal the gate receipts from him and that he would "fight the case to the limit."[34]

The Charleston Sea Gulls were a financial success. According to Ashenbach, "my profits [were] well up in the five figures" in spite of his club's third-place finish. One South Atlantic League scribe wrote, "The Charleston team has been a splendid investment for Ed. Ashenbach. That perpetual smile he wears on the diamond, even when his team is losing, is not hampered any by the knowledge that there is good money in the bank over and above all expenses, made from the grand stand alone, to say nothing of the gate receipts."[35]

According to Ashenbach, the success of the Charleston club and the rest of the league drew the ire of local fans who were against outsiders like him profiting from the game in their region. Eventually the "alien owners" were pressured to sell their clubs in 1905. With city leaders thwarting his efforts and the press criticizing his business practices, he finally sold his franchise on May 20 to a group of local investors "at a very good profit" for $3,500. There may have been unrest within his own clubhouse as well. The *Sporting Life* described him as "a capable base ball man, whose only fault was insubordination on the field." Ashenbach himself recalled, "I will always

---

34. "Mob at the Heels of Ed. Ashenback," *Atlanta Constitution*, August 25, 1904, 3. "Baseball Notes," *Nashua* (NH) *Telegraph*, August 30, 1904, 7. The boys were identified as Claude Gresham and Joe Clarke.

35. "South Atlantic Scraps," *Sporting Life*, July 16, 1904, 21.

be grateful for the little Goddess of Fortune that sent me on my way to Charleston and my penniless investment that turned out so profitably."[36]

Ashenbach returned north and was signed to manage the Scranton (Pennsylvania) Miners in the Class B New York State League the remainder of the 1905 season. While he couldn't reverse their eventual second-division finish, he brought enthusiam to the team and improved their record before season's end. He was brought back in 1906 and made a much better showing, capturing the pennant with an 82-48 record and a 12-game lead over the Albany Senators. The profits his success brought to the team owners renewed his desire to own his own club again. One sportswriter remarked, "He says he is tired of making money for other people."[37]

In the afterglow of a championship season, relations between Ashenbach and Scranton ownership became contentious. He felt the club violated the terms of his contract when it failed to inform him whether he would return in 1907 before the season ended and did not pay him a $500 bonus for the team exceeding $5,000 in profits. The owners insisted that he was already under contract for a second season and they had the right to place him on the club's reserved list. Ashenbach believed the owners would sell his contract to another club without his consent for the

36. *Sporting Life*, June 3, 1905, 17; June 10, 1905, 17. Ashenback, *Humor Among the Minors*, 60. Under local management, the Charleston Sea Gulls (53-70) finished in fourth place, 23½ games behind the Macon Brigands in 1905. According to the *Charleston Courier*, "The attendance began to fall when the fans somehow lost faith in Ashenback. Ashenback saw how things were drifting, and when an offer was made him sold out. But the crowd had been lost, and it was hard to regain it." Quoted in *Sporting Life*, September 30, 1905, 18.

37. *Sporting Life*, July 22, 1905, 19; September 2, 1905, 19; October 7, 1905, 26; September 22, 1906, 14.

highest price possible. As a non-playing manager, he successfully appealed his inclusion on the list to the National Commission that governed organized baseball, enabling him to sign with any club. With this leverage and an offer from the St. Paul, Minnesota club in hand, he countered the Scranton owners' salary increase offer of $3,200 with one that would double his previous salary. Believing the league championship "has given Ashenback such an inflated idea of his worth that he will not even listen to argument," they rejected his proposal and gave him his unconditional release on November 28.[38]

Ashenbach's standing as a successful manager had drawn the attention of the St. Paul Saints and brought him to the highly-regarded American Association in 1907. "Little is known of Ashenback in the West," wrote sportswriter John D. Grant, "but in the East he has the reputation of being one of the best minor league managers in the business, such an eminent authority as Ren Mulford pronouncing him as being worth a carload of the high-class, high-salaried gazabos who are rallying around second division camp fires."[39] To his friend Mulford, Ashenbach was optimistic about his chances to improve on the Saints' seventh-place finish in 1906. "I am not given to boasting, but if I don't take St. Paul into the first

---

38. "High Court Rules," *Sporting Life*, November 10, 1906, 11. "New York League," *Ibid*, November 24, 1906, 8. *Ibid*, December 1, 1906, 7. "Ashenback is Free," *The Sporting News*, December 1, 1906. The Scranton club stated that an audit revealed it had made a profit of $2,500 for the season, which did not meet the requirement for Ashenback to receive his bonus. A local sportswriter contended that Ashenbach's salary-doubling proposal "would wipe out the entire profit of a pennant-winning season, with no margin to go on next year." "New York League," *Sporting Life*, December 1, 1906, 7.

39. "American Association." *Sporting Life*, December 29, 1906, 7.

division next season I'll be willing to dine on crow and pickled buzzard's feet next Thanksgiving."[40]

Unfortunately, he couldn't duplicate his success at Scranton in St. Paul. Despite assembling a roster filled with former major-leaguers, the team finished in last place in the eight-club circuit with a record of 58-96. "Ashenbach did the best he could with the material given him last spring," wrote the *Sporting Life*, "and his administration has been entirely satisfactory to Owner [George] Lennon." There were rumors in August and September during his absence on a scouting trip of his inevitable ouster, which proved to be true. As Ren Mulford wrote, "His St. Paul experience was the first managerial bump he ever sustained."[41]

That same year, he tried unsuccessfully to become a team owner again. In August, he was rumored to be in pursuit of the Dayton, Ohio club in the Class B Central League with Saints second baseman Dick Padden. At the same time, he was reportedly purchasing the Binghampton, New York club in the New York State League with the idea of transferring it northeast to Schenectady. Yet another rumor claimed he and Detroit Tigers third baseman Bill Coughlin had

---

40. "'Ash' and His Saints," *Sporting Life*, December 8, 1906, 10.

41. "American Association News," *Sporting Life*, August 17, 1907, 13. "Condensed Dispatches," *Ibid*, September 7, 1907, 2. "American Association News," *Ibid*, September 21, 1907, 20. After his friend's dismissal, Ren Mulford wrote: "Eddy Ashenbach is recovering from his Saintly experience with the sinners of the Seventh Ward Fishing Club...Ed Ashenbach could put up a stirring lecture[,] 'The Woes of a Tail Ender.'" "Mulfordisms," *Sporting Life*, October 5, 1907, 5.

HUMOR AMONG THE MINORS

acquired the Scranton club. All these reported attempts proved to be unsuccessful.[42]

The previous winter, there had been talk in his hometown that he should be given a chance to manage the Cincinnati Reds. But as one sportswriter remarked a year later, "some of the gilt was cracked off at St. Paul." Many wondered if his colorful antics in the coach's box would work as well in the major leagues, despite the success of similar tactics used by Hughey Jennings of the Detroit Tigers. The writer pointed out that "Ashenbach's one failure is offset by a string of successes...Nevertheless nobody has whispered the name of Ashenbach in Red Society since the pumpkins began to ripen." Despite his success in the minors, Ashenbach would never get the opportunity to prove himself in the majors.[43]

In August 1908, while managing the fifth-place Johnstown (Pennsylvania) Johnnies[44] in the Class B Tri-State League, a story circulated that Ashenbach had been hired as a coach and scout by the World champion Chicago Cubs. "Ashenback is one of the best coaches in the country," the report stated. "It is believed his inspiring manner will cause the Cubs to win games they might otherwise lose." Manager Frank Chance denied the report, saying that he didn't need non-playing coaches and derisively added, "Moreover,

---

42. *Washington* (D.C.) *Herald*, August 26, 1907, 6. "Ashenbach's Scheme," *Sporting Life*, August 10, 1907, 23. "Binghampton Briefs," *Ibid*, August 17, 1907, 15. "Baseball Notes," *Washington* (D.C.) *Herald*, November 10, 1907, 4. *Washington* D.C. *Times*, November 13, 1907, 10.

43. "Then and Now," *Sporting Life*, December 7, 1907, 7.

44. Ashenbach was fined $50 by the Tri-State League that season for promising under-the-table money to a pitcher named Baxter. "Tri-State League," *Sporting Life*, June 16, 1909, 8.

the National League would not stand for Ashenbach's work on the [coaching] lines for a moment."[45]

Ashenbach stayed in the Tri-State League and took over the helm of the Altoona (Pennsylvania) Mountaineers in 1909, leading them to a fourth-place finish. Afterward, he criticized the league's salary limit that prevented higher-class players from being signed, resulting in less experienced players on the field and low attendance around the league. "Why[,] do you know in Williamsport one game last summer we had seven real, live spectators that included the policemen and the groundtender," he said after the season. "You think that is bad, but it could have been worse."[46]

Ashenbach returned to the New York State League in 1910 where he enjoyed his greatest success four years earlier and spent his last two seasons piloting the Syracuse (New York) Stars. Despite his assurances that his club would finish in the first division, it was mired in sixth place in early July with an overworked four-man pitching staff and undisciplined players. "Manager Ashenbach is evidently having trouble with his players," noted one sportswriter, "and [he] has added another to the rules which must be observed. The new addition requires that players be at the hotel at 11 o'clock when on the road. A pretty stiff fine will be attached to those who fail to abide by this ruling. Harry Aubrey, shortstop of the Syracuse team, has been indefinitely suspended by Manager Ashenbach

45. "Ashenback's Latest," *Sporting Life*, August 15, 1908, 2. "Tri-State Artist Will Join the Champions," *Ibid*, August 8, 1908, 9. "Ashenbach Not to Join Champions," *Pittsburgh Press*, August 14, 1908, 15. Apparently the story started after a visit to Johnstown by Cubs owner Charles W. Murphy, who met with Ashenbach about acquiring left-handed pitcher Floyd Kroh. Murphy, who was also from Cincinnati, joked that Ashenbach's unique coaching abilities could be used in Chicago. *Ibid*.

46. "Ashenback Says Limit Kills League," *Trenton* [NJ] *True American*, December 15, 1909, 7.

HUMOR AMONG THE MINORS

for alleged indifferent playing."[47] But he managed to reverse the struggling club's fortunes (helped in large part by 29-game winner and future Hall of Fame pitcher Grover Cleveland Alexander) and elevated it into second place by early September. The Stars finished with a record of 78-57, five-and-a-half games behind the pennant-winning Wilkes-Barre Barons.[48]

Even with a first-division club and a successful season nearing its end, Ashenbach felt that it would be his last. "He is getting tired of the constant grind and strain," the *Sporting Life* reported, "and as he has plenty of money saved up, he will go into some other business in the Fall, according to his present plans." Yet three months later, he signed a contract to guide the team once again.[49]

Throughout his career, Ashenbach was known for his wit and humor both on and off the field. He entertained sportswriters and fans alike with stories of life in the minor leagues, many of which had never appeared in print. Having been in baseball for 20 years, he had amassed quite a collection. In January 1911, it was reported that he and *Cincinnati Enquirer* sportswriter Jack Ryder were collaborating on a new book tentatively entitled *Minor League Stars*. "'Ash' says the fans are getting tired of reading about big league stars," it noted.[50] Two months later, its publication was announced with a revised title.

> "Humor Among the Minors" is the title of a new book published by the noted minor league manager, Ed. Ashenbach, aided by

---

47. "Syracuse's Sad Story," *Sporting Life*, July 9, 1910, 19.
48. "Ashenbach Strengthens His Stars," *Sporting Life*, September 3, 1910, 21.
49. *Sporting Life*, August 13, 1910, 21. *Trenton* [N.J.] *True American*, November 17, 1910, 7.
50. *Sporting Life*, January 7, 1911, 26.

Jack Ryder of the Cincinnati "Enquirer." This book contains a fund of entertaining and amusing anecdotes, together with funny experiences, gathered by Manager Ashenbach during a checkered career of 20 years on the diamond. There are valuable tables incorporated into the book, showing the mileage of all important base ball leagues in the United States and Canada. This particular feature alone makes the book worth its price, $1.00, to any base ball man. This book appeals alike to professional base ball players and base ball "fans." It is printed from large, clear type on a superior quality of paper and embraces over 300 pages of text. In addition it contains 16 halftone portraits of important base ball characters. It is published by M. A. Donahue & Co., 415 Dearborn Street, Chicago, and is for sale by all booksellers and sporting goods houses.[51]

Ashenbach received considerable press coverage for the book with his claim to have originated the term "bonehead." He recalled first using it to describe a teammate nicknamed "Zeekoe" (Ashenbach never identified him), a catcher with the 1897 Springfield Governors who had difficulty with high foul pop-ups. During a game, Zeekoe circled under one "doing his sky-dance, under it," as Ashenbach described, when the ball dropped onto his exposed head and bounced thirty feet into the stands. "The blow would have felled an ox," he wrote, but Zeekoe picked up his mask and went back behind the plate unphased. That evening, while the catcher ate his meal, Ashenbach put his

---

51. *Sporting Life*, March 11, 1911, 4.

hands on his teammate's head searching for the inevitable bump. Not finding one, he told another teammate, Joseph Reilly, "No wonder, Josh, that he isn't hurt. His head is of solid bone." Ashenbach wrote in his book, "Ever since that night I have applied the expression 'bonehead' to any player guilty of unusual stupidity, and it has gained wide circulation."[52]

As *Humor Among the Minors* made its debut in the spring of 1911, Ashenbach had decided against retirement and returned to the Syracuse Stars. It turned out to be a mistake. The team struggled and blame was directed at him by the local press, displeased fans in the largest city in the league, and his own disgruntled players. On the first of July, he confessed that he was "unable to make them play ball." Hard feelings were further embittered by the fact that he could not be removed as manager without being paid his full salary for the entire season, a costly proposition for team owners. Nevertheless, he was fired on July 6. Although he threatened a lawsuit to recoup his full salary, he agreed to a settlement and returned to his home in Cincinnati.[53]

It was believed Ashenbach had suffered a nervous breakdown before his firing.[54] The Cincinnati Reds offered him a scouting position for the remainder of the season, which he accepted. One of the last stories he shared took place at this time. While scouting players in the Blue Grass League, he thought it best to be unseen by rivals from other clubs and decided

---

52. Ashenback, *Humor Among the Minors*, 74–75. The origin of "bonehead" was discussed previously in Bozeman Bugler, "The Bonehead," *New York Tribune*, July 3, 1910.

53. *Syracuse Herald*, July 2, 1911. *Sporting Life*, July 15, 1911, 1. *Ibid*, 24.

54. Ashenbach's nervous breakdown at Syracuse is mentioned in "Game's Clown May Lose Mind," *Milwaukee Journal*, January 6, 1912, and "Ed Ashenbach is Dead," *Toledo News*, February 17, 1912.

to watch from a hill that overlooked the field. When he reached the top, he literally stumbled on Cleveland scout Bob Gilks, who was lying hidden in the tall grass. Ashenbach lost his balance and fell downhill, where his fall was broken by St. Louis scout Billy Doyle, who was at the bottom making his own hiding place under the bleachers.[55]

Ashenbach's mental health worsened over the next several months until he became bedridden in November. He suffered from hallucinations and believed he was still coaching his team, using such expressions as "Go it, boy!" "Slide and you're safe!" "One little bingle now!" One Cincinnati report attributed his condition to writing his book. "He has been in poor health since he published his book, 'Humor of the Minors [sic],'" it stated, "and it is believed that the strain of his literary efforts is the cause..." He was diagnosed with paresis (paralysis associated with a mental disorder) and committed by a judge's order to Longview Hospital, a mental health facility in Cincinnati, on January 27, 1912.[56]

Upon learning of his condition, Washington Senators manager Clark Griffith said, "I am sorry to hear of the fate of poor Ed Ashenbach. He is one of the most experienced managers in the business, and is known personally by thousands of players, all of whom are hoping for a speedy recovery from the disease which has affected his mind."[57]

---

55. "National League Notes," *Sporting Life*, August 5, 1911, 9. "Edward Ashenback's Last Baseball Yard," *Chester* (PA) *Times*, March 4, 1912.

56. *Milwaukee Journal*, January 6, 1912. "Ashenback in Hospital," *The Sunday Times* (Charleston, SC), January 28, 1912. *The Sporting News*, February 22, 1912, 2. "Ed. Ashenback Has Paresis," *Trenton* (NJ) *True American*, January 16, 1912, 7.

57. *Washington* [D.C.] *Times*, January 29, 1912, 10.

HUMOR AMONG THE MINORS

Unfortunately, Ashenbach never recovered. "The mind that invented so many witty sayings and amused so many...began to weaken," said the *Sporting Life*. "It was a blank when the end came in an asylum in Cincinnati."[58] He died at Longview Hospital at 1:30 P.M. on February 12, 1912. He was 40 years old.

His wife Lillie believed he may have been abused while under the hospital's care, citing a wound at the back of his head and several missing teeth. A coroner's inquest six days later determined that the wound was old and the cause of death was pneumonia. (His death certificate filed the day before attributed it to "dementia paralytic.") "Doctors and attendants at the hospital testified that Ashenbach was very violent, and that they were forced to strap him down on several occasions," it was revealed. "They denied, however, that he received any injury at their hands which might have caused his death."[59]

Edward Ashenbach was laid to rest on February 19 at Cincinnati's St. Mary Cemetery. He left behind his wife Lillie and 17-year-old son Edward H. Ashenbach. "The world is really better off for Ashenbach's life," eulogized longtime friend Ben Mulford, Jr. "He brightened all the shadows with his optimistic personality until disease robbed him of the quality which made him the life of every party of which he was a member. It is hard to comprehend the tragedy of his end—the loss of a mind that always saw the bright side. God rest his soul!"[60]

Kevin D. McCann

58. "Ashenbach Dead," *Sporting Life*, February 24, 1912, 8.
59. Edward Ashenbach Death Certificate, 1912. Ohio Deaths, 1908-1953, http://familysearch.org. *Washington* [D.C.] *Times*, February 18, 1912, 1. *Sporting Life*, March 2, 1912, 8.
60. *Sporting Life*, March 2, 1912, 10.

Qualifications for a Manager.

BY EDWARD ASHENBACH.[1]

Be a fighter. Never lose your head. Don't try to bulldoze the umpire. Be witty and sarcastic.

Mix with your men, but never lose their respect. Lay down no rules, but give to understand certain unwritten laws must be abided by. Have your men up and fighting all the time. Never give up.

Don't be afraid to let out your voice in coaching.

Don't follow the horses.

---

1. "Handy Precepts for Managers," *Washington* (D.C.) *Times*, May 17, 1907, 10.

Edward Michael (Ed, Eddie) Ashenbach
Born October 18, 1871, Cincinnati, Ohio. Died February 16, 1912, Cincinnati, Ohio.

Year	Club	League	Pos	G	AB	R	H	2B	3B	HR	SB	BA
1890	Canton	Tri-State	RF-CF-SS	7	21	1	4	2	0	0	0	.190
1891					Did not play professional ball							
1892	Harrisburg/Allentown	Pennsylvania State	OF-SS	58	220	25	43	4	2	1	9	.195
1893	Canton	Ohio-Michigan	P-1B	4	15	1	4	0	0	0	1	.267
1894	Atlanta	Southern	OF	33	118	20	24	6	2	0	6	.203
	Altoona/Reading/Shenandoah	Pennsylvania State	OF-1B-P	53	210	41	54	4	3	3	—	.257
1895	Dallas	Texas-Southern	OF	115	486	106	152	28	3	6	23	.313
1896	Dallas	Texas-Southern	OF	71	295	44	76	13	4	1	29	.258
	Paterson	Atlantic	OF	3	12	2	2	0	0	0	0	.167
1897	Fort Worth/Houston	Texas Association	OF	61	224	48	57	—	—	—	16	.254
	Springfield, OH	Inter-State	OF	67	263	50	76	9	4	2	16	.289
1898	New Castle	Inter-State	OF	149	569	97	160	31	10	1	23	.281
1899	New Castle	Inter-State	OF	29	117	16	23	5	0	0	6	.197
	Schenectady	New York State	OF	54	198	32	60	6	3	0	13	.303

Year	Team (role)	League	Position	G	AB	R	H	2B	3B	HR	SB	BA
1900	Hampton (player/mgr)/Norfolk	Virginia	OF-P-1B-C	56	213	36	49	6	3	1	22	.230
1901	Newport News-Hampton/Tarboro (manager)	Virginia–North Carolina	OF-C-P-1B	66	227	32	52	5	2	1	6	.229
	Sacramento	California	1B-OF	19	67	10	11	2	1	0	2	.164
1902	Charlotte (manager)	North Carolina			Statistics unavailable							
	Shreveport (manager)	Southern Assoc.	OF	13	46	2	10	2	0	0	1	.217
1903	Nashua (manager)	New England	OF-P	60	190	25	47	2	0	2	7	.247
	Evansville (manager)	Central	OF	12	37	5	12	—	—	—	—	.324
1904	Charleston (manager)	South Atlantic	OF-1B	52	157	15	38	—	—	—	—	.242
1905	Charleston (manager)	South Atlantic			Statistics unavailable							
	Scranton (manager)	New York State	P-OF	6	9	1	4	0	0	0	0	.444
1906	Scranton (manager)	New York State	1B-OF	2	1	0	0	0	0	0	0	.000
1907	St. Paul (manager)	American Assoc.			Non-playing manager							
1908	Johnstown (manager)	Tri-State			Non-playing manager							
1909	Altoona (manager)	Tri-State			Non-playing manager							
1910	Syracuse (manager)	New York State			Non-playing manager							
1911	Syracuse (manager)	New York State			Non-playing manager							
21 pro seasons	**Career totals (incomplete)**			990	3,796	609	958	125	37	18	180	.252

Humor Among the Minors

True Tales From the Baseball Brush

EDWARD MICHAEL ASHENBACK

Humor Among the Minors

TRUE TALES FROM THE BASEBALL BRUSH

BY
EDWARD MICHAEL ASHENBACK
*Manager of the Syracuse Club of the
New York State League*

EDITED BY
JACK RYDER
Baseball Editor of the Cincinnati Enquirer

COVER CARTOON BY
CLAUDE SHAFER
*Sporting Cartoonist of the Cincinnati Enquirer
and originator of "Old Man Grump"*

HALFTONES BY
THE MODERN ENGRAVING COMPANY
OF CINCINNATI

PUBLISHED BY
M. A. DONOHUE & COMPANY
CHICAGO

FULLY COPYRIGHTED BY
EDWARD MICHAEL ASHENBACK
AND
JACK RYDER
1911

Play Ball

INTRODUCTION

NO baseball man outside of the major leagues is better or more widely known than Edward Michael Ashenback, who has played ball and managed teams for the past twenty years in the North, South, East and West. Equipped with an unusual sense of humor and a retentive memory, Mr. Ashenback has never failed to see the funny side of his numerous baseball experiences and to note the many entertaining episodes which have come under his observation, and in many of which he has had an active part. The result is this volume, consisting of true and original stories involving the early careers of many noted players. Every tale in the book is authentic and the history of an actual experience. In addition to a large number of anecdotes, there have been incorporated some interesting data, including a brief history of the National Association of Minor Leagues, a sample contract such as every minor league ballplayer is required to sign, a good deal of sage advice for players and fans, and other matters of information for the baseball public. An original feature is the set of tables giving the correct mileage between the cities of all the leagues in the country, something which has never before been published, and will prove of great value to managers who are arranging exhibition tours, or are figuring on their traveling expenses for the season.

The volume is dedicated to the players of the United States and the fans of the hundreds of minor league cities in the commonwealth.

JACK RYDER.

JACK RYDER
Baseball Editor Cincinnati Enquirer

Career of a Cincinnati Boy.

A RESULT of perseverance and the habit of keeping after a desired object until he gets it, is Mr. Ed Ashenback, King of the Minors. From the moment that Ed was old enough to earn a nickel by running an errand, he began hoarding coin, with the sole object of becoming a baseball magnate. By the time he had amassed fifteen cents, his shoes, number eight, children's size, were worn out, but instead of purchasing fresh footgear, he dashed madly to a sporting goods store and invested in a juvenile baseball. He wore white kid gloves all summer, the same that he had on when he made his entrance into the world on October 18, 1871. Though slightly soiled by hard usage, they served his purpose so well that in a course of a few months he was able to secure a bat and a glove. With these spurs to his ambition he worked faithfully, practicing daily whenever the other boys would let him. Even in the winter he would refuse to stop. One day he was sent into the woodshed to get a mess of kindlings. Soon the sounds of a series of hard bumps resounded through the house. A familiar face appeared at the door of the woodshed and Ed was discovered with a section of hickory sapling and a knot about the size of a baseball, with which he was practicing hitting flies to the outfield. "What in the world are you doing, Eddie?" was the astonished question. ''Saying nothing, but sawing wood," replied the future magnate. Since that time he has said more, but he has never failed to saw wood.

In climbing the ladder of baseball fame Mr. Ashenback became a connoisseur of hard knocks. Every time he tried to reach a higher round some one above him would step on his hands. But pride and perseverance kept him at it, and today he is proud of the broken and crooked fingers, which resulted from his strenuous climb.

It was as a catcher that Mr. Ashenback started out to realize his ambition. He and George Hogriever, another Cincinnati boy, used to do most of their practicing together, because they were such poor players that the other boys would not let them in the regular game. But Ed was always on hand. Sometimes only eight members of the Millcreek Bottoms team would show up, and he would get a chance to break in. When the regular nine were all there Ed and ' 'Hoggie" would go behind the backstop and practice together, hoping that somebody would be hurt so that they could butt in. Perseverance was rewarded and Ed finally became the regular catcher of the old Bond Hill team and the Manhattans. League managers, blind to their best interests, failed to wire him for his terms, and he wore out the chairs of the different newspaper offices, sitting around in the evening hoping to hear of a job with some professional team. Finally Ren Mulford, the famous authority on the game, in order to get rid of this persistent young man, persuaded the manager of the Canton team, in the old Tri-State League, to give him a trial. This was a step up the ladder and Ed gladly accepted the magnificent offer of fifty dollars per month to catch for Canton. The now famous Cy Young was pitching for Canton that year, and Ed was put in to catch him the day he joined the team. The result of Cy's speed was disastrous. His inshoot developed a habit of going on through to the backstop, carrying Ed's mitt along with it. Running 90 feet for his glove after every pitched ball was a bit hard on the new catcher, but it was a blessing in disguise. It showed the manager the speed of the new recruit. and the next day he was sent to center field, far from Cy's maddening shoots. There he finished the season, not, indeed, with eclat, but still with the same old brand of perseverance.

When Ash returned to Cincinnati at the close of the season, he met Tom Loftus, at that time manager of the Reds, who were in a bad way for pitchers. "I know one that you could use," said Mr. Ashenback, the professional ball player, in his purest Bohemian patois; "his name is Denton T. Young, and they call him the Tuscarawas Railsplitter. He is a terror. All that and more. Lasso him quickly, for he has so much speed that he will get away if you don't sign him in a hurry."

This was good dope, but, as usual, Tom Loftus was beaten to it. Pat Tebeau signed Cy for his Cleveland team, and the next week the Tuscarawas Railsplitter shut out the famous White Stockings of Chicago in his first game in big league company.

Ed did not go back to Canton in 1891, but stayed in Cincinnati making scissors in a hardware factory. This illustrates his keen foresight, as he has had considerable use for the shears in late years, cutting coupons, as well as favorable notices of his managerial ability out of the newspapers.

After a year's rest Mr. Ashenback again started upon his climb up the ladder of baseball fame. In 1892-1893 he was with the Allentown team of the Pennsylvania League. Having passed up backstop work he devoted himself to cavorting around in the outfield, and assisting in getting his fellow runners around the circuit by his labors on the coaching lines. In this department Ash developed great ability. Only pitchers with callous feelings and nerves of iron were able to stand his good-natured Fliegende-blaetter conversation. All tender souls went up in the air so far that the Allentowns had the game roped, thrown and tied before they came down. As his conversational ability did not interfere with his midfield cavorting and inside work, Ash soon acquired a reputation that attracted the attention of Ted Sullivan, the inventor of more new leagues than any man under the sun. Ted came over to Allentown to see him play, and one view of Ash on the coaching line was enough for him. He grabbed the monologue artist in a hurry, and for the next four years these two interesting characters worked together. Ted took Ash to Atlanta, in the Southern League, with him in 1894, and in 1895 to Dallas, Texas, where the Cincinnati boy played three years. Wearying of the South, which is too warm for the rich German blood that dashes furiously through his veins, Ash went to Springfield, Ohio, in the Inter-State League in 1898, and the following year to New Castle, Pa., in the same organization.

Branches Out As A Mogul.

All this time the keen wit of the lad had been laying the foundation for higher things. He had early made up his mind not to remain a mere player forever, and in 1900 the chance came to him to take another forward step. Rather he manufactured the chance by going east and organizing the Virginia League. From a center-fielder he became a promoter. Ash took the Hampton franchise of the new league, an act of great generosity, for Hampton consisted of one house which was attached to a freight car and was usually moved away on the days his team was scheduled to play at home. The admiring throng of Hampton usually consisted of Mr. Ashenback and a couple of substitute players. Not even Ed's nerve could carry the league through the season, and he brought back to Cincinnati more experience than cash. But he had discovered another great pitcher in Christy Mathewson, just out of Bucknell College, who was drawing ninety dollars a month from Norfolk in the shattered Virginia League. Ed recommended him in strong German accents to the Red management, and actually succeeded in getting him signed, but John T. Brush let him get away to his dear friend, Mr. Andrew Freedman, of New York. It is not the fault of Ed Ashenback that Cy Young and Matty are not winning world's championships for Redland now. He picked up these two great stars when they were in the rough and did all he could to land them for the Reds.

Unabashed by the breaking up of his baby league in 1900 Ash went back the following year and organized the Virginia-North Carolina League, taking the Newport News franchise. Still the territory was unripe and the league died a natural death in August. Arthur Devlin, of the Giants, and the late Jimmy Sebring made their professional debut in this little league. After burying the remains and shedding a few tears at the grave Ash made up his mind to corral some good players for a major league club in the capacity of a scout and for that purpose went out to the Pacific Coast. His budding fame had preceded him and he was urged to accept the management of the Sacramento club, which he did, remaining with them until the close of the season.

From that time Ash's career has been one of continued and increasing success as a manager and a magnate. In 1902 he organized the North Carolina League and took hold of the Charlotte club, where his clever management proved the destruction of the organization. His club broke a world's record for winning consecutive games. The team won twenty-five straight games, which was too much for the other clubs to swallow, and broke up the League. Ash finished the season as manager of the Shreveport, La., team of the Southern League.

In 1903 Ash went to the New England League and lost the pennant on the very last day of the season with his Nashua, N. H., club. However, the old fever to be a magnate still remained, for he again went south and organized that snug little South-Atlantic League. Ash selected the city of Charleston, which proved a real gold mine. With the profits running well up into double figures and a strong feeling prevailing against alien ownership down in

Dixie, Ash was obliged to dispose of his interests in the Charleston club, which he did at an enormously profitable figure on May 20, 1905. On June 13 he took charge of the Scranton club of the New York State League. He found the affairs of the club in miserable shape, the team being a hopeless last in the race. By dint of hard work and an entire reorganization of the team, Ash finished in sixth place, and not only wiped out a heavy indebtedness but closed the season with a neat profit.

In 1906 Ash won the pennant, hands down, in Scranton. The team had such a lead by the fourth of July that the attendance fell off wofully, the patrons having formed the conclusion that the Scranton club would win with ease.

The year following the St. Paul club of the American Association weaned Ash away from his great success, and it was at St. Paul that he met his first reverses, his club finishing a hopeless last in the race. Nothing daunted, Ash went to the Tri-State League, and his Johnstown and Altoona clubs finished well up in the race. At Syracuse last season his club was defeated for the pennant during the last week of the season, and but for accidents he would have added another pennant to his string.

A Persistent Hustler.

Ed Ashenback's career is a living illustration of the success which follows a game, persistent fight along fixed lines toward a certain ambitious goal. Hard knocks have been spurs to his perseverance. From the start he was up against it, but the obstacles that could not be pushed aside he dashed over or around. Never a wonderful player, he more than made up in intelligence, in activity and in constant work for his team's interests, what he lacked in actual playing ability. For ten years he played professional ball on a salary, but never for a moment did he lose sight of his ambition to become a leader rather than a follower. The difficulties of promoting new leagues never phased him. He organized the Virginia, the Virginia-North Carolina and the South Atlantic Leagues only to see the two former go up in hot air before the season was over. "Never mind," said Ash, "there are other leagues," and he kept on hustling.

Today he is ranked as one of the best minor league managers in the country. He has a comfortable wad stowed away in the faithful sock and a delightful new home in the aristocratic suburb of Avondale, the door of which wouldn't know a wolf if it saw one. Better still he has a warm heart, a helping hand and a sense of humor. As a story-teller, Magnate Ashenback has had no equal since Chauncey M. Depew retired from public life. He has been called eccentric, but his eccentricities are governed by reason and are effective in his business. Ed's wheels work for Mr. Ashenback. As he himself says: "I am never so mad as not to know what to do next." He is a fine example of the result of persistent hustling, and a credit to Redland, which has always been and always will be his favorite spot on earth.

JACK RYDER.

AUGUST HERRMANN
Chairman of the National Commission

The National Association.

IN the years 1900 and 1901, when the American League entered the field against that great old organization, the National League, matters pertaining to the small clubs were indeed distressing. Players of ability whom either one of the major organizations desired were taken from the minors without any redress whatsoever. Chaos seemed to reign supreme among the small clubs all over the country. There were hundreds of thousands of dollars invested in clubs throughout the land, with little or no protection for the club-owners. However, it must not be believed that all this time the small-fry were lying idle. Not on your life, for on September 6, 1901, there met a body of men at Chicago who fairly revolutionized the situation. The brains of minor league balldom met at this meeting and concentrated their every effort to gain their just dues. They elected for President P. T. Powers, then acting in that capacity for the Eastern League; J. H. Farrell of Auburn, N. Y., as Secretary; and T. H. Murnane, Pres. of the New England League, W. H. Lucas, Pres. of the Northwestern League, Judge W. M. Kavanaugh, Pres. of the Southern League, and James H. O'Rourke of the Connecticut League as members of the National Board. These officials represented the very cream of the baseball intellect of the minor leagues throughout the country. I can best present to you the words of my esteemed friend, Mr. Jos. Flanner, at that time editor of the St. Louis *Sporting News*, who three years later at St. Louis paid the officers the following compliments:

"The election of P. T. Powers as President of the National Association of Minor Leagues, J. H. Farrell as Secretary, and M. H. Sexton, Judge Wm. M. Kavanaugh, W. H. Lucas, T. H. Murnane, and James H. O'Rourke as members of the National Board, assures the National Association a successful administration of its affairs. Powers, able, alert, affable, makes an ideal presiding officer, and his past record is proof of his executive qualifications. Farrell, industrious, courteous and penetrating, is the wheelhorse of the minor leagues. Sexton, shrewd, well-balanced and fearless, Kavanaugh, never obtrusive, but always prominent, Lucas, reticent, but reliable and zealous, Murnane and O'Rourke, both graduates from the players' ranks, and as prominent in their present profession as when popular idols, constitute a tribunal that any organization might well feel proud of. Any case presented to this Board is decided on its merits and rarely is there a difference of opinion. As a rule, the points submitted to Sec. Farrell for decision are passed on by only three members. The papers are first sent to Mr. Murnane and are transmitted without endorsement to Mr. O'Rourke, who forms his conclusions and forwards them to Mr. Kavanaugh or Mr. Sexton. It is a compliment to both gentlemen to say that during their long service there has never been a variance in the views of Mr. Murnane and Mr. O'Rourke on questions submitted to them. Each without consulting the other, mails his opinion to Sec. Farrell, who refers to the uniformity of their findings in complimentary terms."

Such is the caliber of the men chosen by the minor league delegates to represent their interests. When the National and American Leagues buried the hatchet the National Board lost no time in presenting to both leagues an agreement that was accepted at once by both leagues. This little acorn, planted at that memorable meeting in Chicago with a membership of scarcely a dozen clubs, has since then grown into a giant in stature. No less than 50 leagues are now members of this powerful organization. M. H. Sexton is now the able president of the Association. In Sec. Farrell's last report he says:

"The National Association has outstripped all previous membership records. Banded together throughout the United States and Canada with unity of thought and purpose for the universal protection and betterment of Minor Leagues, who can adequately measure its strength for the general good of baseball? Fifty League organizations, embracing 336 cities and towns in America and Canada, qualified for membership in 1910.

2,346 telegrams were received and 1,787 were transmitted by this office.

10,145 players' contracts were received, recorded and promulgated.

1,673 "Terms Accepted" were examined and promulgated.

2,155 players were reported released by purchase between the National Association clubs.

291 optional agreements were approved.

171 optional agreements were exercised.

3,291 players were reported to this office for release.

859 players were suspended.

262 players were reinstated.

12,600 copies of the official bulletin were mailed from this office during the current year.

605 disputed and contested cases were passed upon, and decisions handed down.

153 cases are on hand ready for decision, making a grand total of 758 cases handled during the year.

Number of players drafted by the National League—70.

Number of players drafted by the American League—68.

Number of players drafted by the National Association—130.

Total amount received through this office for drafted players (and money refunded on drafts disallowed):

National League	$46,700
American League	37,800
National Association	58,000
Total	$143,200
Amount paid on optional agreements	43,600
Amount paid for release by purchase for National Association players:	152,000
Grand Total, received through this office for drafted players, optional agreement players and released by purchase players	338,800

JOHN E. BRUCE
Secretary of the National Commission

In transacting the business of the Association, together with the collecting of evidence in disputed cases, correspondence with players, managers, club-owners, directors, League secretaries, and League Presidents, 20,177 letters were handled by this office."

Mr. Farrell further states that the following organizations have qualified for membership for the season of 1911:

CLASS A

THE AMERICAN ASSOCIATION: T. M. Chivington, President, Chicago, Ill.
  MEMBERS: Minneapolis, St. Paul, Columbus, Indianapolis, Louisville, Toledo, Kansas City and Milwaukee.
THE EASTERN LEAGUE: Ed. Barrow, President, New York.
  MEMBERS: Baltimore, Newark, Jersey City, Rochester, Buffalo, Montreal, Toronto and Providence.
THE PACIFIC COAST LEAGUE: Thos. F. Graham, President, San Francisco, Cal.
  MEMBERS: San Francisco, Oakland, Los Angeles, Vernon, Sacramento, Portland.
THE WESTERN LEAGUE: N. L. O'Neil, President, Chicago, Ill.
  MEMBERS: Denver, Sioux City, St. Joseph, Lincoln, Des Moines, Topeka, Omaha and Wichita, Kan.
THE SOUTHERN LEAGUE: Judge Wm. M. Kavanaugh, President, Little Rock, Ark.

MEMBERS: New Orleans, Atlanta, Montgomery, Mobile, Memphis, Nashville, Birmingham and Chattanooga.

CLASS B

NEW YORK STATE LEAGUE: John H. Farrell, President, Auburn, N. Y.
MEMBERS: Syracuse, Utica, Binghamton, Scranton, Wilkesbarre, Elmira, Troy and Albany.
THE CONNECTICUT LEAGUE: J. H. O'Rourke, Secretary, Bridgeport, Conn.
MEMBERS: Bridgeport, New Britain, New Haven, Hartford, Waterbury, Holyoke, Springfield, and Northampton.
THE CENTRAL LEAGUE: Dr. F. R. Carson, President, South Bend, Ind.
MEMBERS: Dayton, Ft. Wayne, South Bend, Grand Rapids, Wheeling, Zanesville, Evansville, Terre Haute.
THE NEW ENGLAND LEAGUE: T. H. Murnane, President, Boston, Mass.
MEMBERS: Lowell, Lawrence, Haverhill, Brockton, Fall River, New Bedford, Lynn and Worcester.
THE NORTHWESTERN LEAGUE: R. H. Lindsay, President, Seattle, Wash.
MEMBERS: Spokane, Seattle, Tacoma, and Vancouver.
TRI-STATE LEAGUE: Charles F. Carpenter, President, Altoona, Pa.
MEMBERS: Johnstown, Altoona, Harrisburg,

Trenton, Lancaster, Reading, York and Williamsport.

THE THREE-EYE LEAGUE: A. R. Tearney, President, Chicago, Ill.

MEMBERS: Waterloo, Peoria, Danville, Dubuque, Rock Island, Davenport, Bloomington, Springfield.

CLASS C

WESTERN ASSOCIATION: J. H. Shaw, President, Enid, Okla.

MEMBERS: Springfield, Mo., Muskogee, El Reno, Sapulpa, Guthrie, and Enid, Okla.

WESTERN CANADA LEAGUE: C. J. Eckstrom, President, Lethbridge, Alta.

MEMBERS: Medicine Hat, Moose Jaw, Calgary, Edmonton, Winnipeg, Brandon, Lethbridge and Regina.

THE OHIO AND PENNSYLVANIA LEAGUE: G. L. Moreland, President, Pittsburg, Pa.

MEMBERS: Youngstown, Akron, Erie, Mansfield, New Castle, McKeesport, East Liverpool, and Canton.

SOUTH ATLANTIC LEAGUE: W. R. Joyner, President, Atlanta, Ga.

MEMBERS: Charleston, Albany, Macon, Columbus, Jacksonville, Columbia, Augusta, and Savannah. Ga.

THE VIRGINIA LEAGUE: C. R. Williams, President, Roanoke, Va.

MEMBERS: Richmond, Norfolk, Portsmouth, Danville, Lynchburg, and Roanoke.

THE TEXAS LEAGUE: W. P. Allen, President, Austin, Texas.
MEMBERS: San Antonio, Galveston, Houston, Waco, Shreveport, Ft. Worth, Dallas and Oklahoma City, Okla.

CLASS D

THE KANSAS LEAGUE: P. H. Hostutler, President, Hutchinson, Kan.
MEMBERS: Great Bend, Hutchinson, Newton, Larned, Lyons, McPherson, Arkansas City and Wellington.
THE BLUE GRASS LEAGUE OF KENTUCKY: Dr. W. C. Ussery, President, Paris, Ky.
MEMBERS: Lexington, Maysville, Paris, Winchester, Richmond and Hopkinsville.
THE COTTON STATES LEAGUE: A. C. Crowder, President, Jackson, Miss.
MEMBERS: Vicksburg, Jackson, Yazoo City, Hattiesburg and Greenwood, Miss.
CENTRAL KANSAS LEAGUE: J. H. Kraemer, President, Ada, Kan.
MEMBERS: Ellsworth, Abilene, Junction City, Clay Center, Beloit, Minneapolis, Salina and Manhattan.
MINNESOTA-WISCONSIN LEAGUE: J. A. Elliot, President, La Crosse, Wis.
MEMBERS: La Crosse, Eau Claire, Wausau, Superior, Wis., Duluth, Winona, Red Wing, and Rochester, Minn.
NORTHERN STATE LEAGUE OF INDIANA: C. W. Halderman, President, Marion, Ind.

MEMBERS: Marion, Bluffton, Kokomo, Wabash, LaFayette and Huntington.

NORTHEAST-ARKANSAS LEAGUE: J. R. Bertig, President, Jonesboro, Ark.

MEMBERS: Jonesboro, Paragould, Caruthersville, and Marianna.

THE WISCONSIN-ILLINOIS LEAGUE: Chas. F. Moll, President, Milwaukee, Wis.

MEMBERS: Green Bay, Oshkosh, Freeport, Rockford, Ill., Madison, Fond du Lac, Appleton and Racine, Wis.

THE SOUTHERN-MICHIGAN ASSOCIATION: J. F. Bowen, President, Saginaw, Mich.

MEMBERS: Saginaw, Flint, Lansing, Adrian, Kalamazoo, Battle Creek, Bay City and Jackson.

THE CENTRAL ASSOCIATION: M. E. Justice, President, Keokuk, Iowa.

MEMBERS: Burlington, Ottumwa, Keokuk, Hannibal, Jacksonville, Waterloo, Kewanee and Quincy.

OHIO STATE LEAGUE: R. W. Read, President, Columbus, Ohio.

MEMBERS: Lima, Newark, Portsmouth, Lancaster, Mansfield and Marion.

ILLINOIS-MISSOURI LEAGUE: A. E. Blain, President, Canton, Ill.

MEMBERS: Macomb, Galesburg, Monmouth, Canton, Pekin and Beardstown.

EASTERN CAROLINA LEAGUE: Dr. Joel Whitaker, President, Raleigh, N. C.

MEMBERS: Raleigh, Wilson, Wilmington, Goldsboro, Rocky Mount, Fayetteville.

CAROLINA ASSOCIATION: J. H. Wearn, President, Charlotte, N. C.
MEMBERS: Greenville, Spartanburg, Charlotte, Winston-Salem, Anderson, and Greensboro.

SOUTHWEST-TEXAS BASEBALL LEAGUE: B. S. Dickinson, President, Austin, Tex.
MEMBERS: Corpus Christi, Brownsville, Bay City, Beeville, Laredo, Victoria.

SOUTHEASTERN LEAGUE: E. B. Fisher, Secretary, Morristown, Tenn.
MEMBERS: Asheville, N. C., Johnson City, Morristown, Knoxville, Tenn., Rome, Ga., Gadsden, Ala.

MICHIGAN-STATE LEAGUE: E. W. Dickerson, President, Grand Rapids, Mich.
MEMBERS: Holland, Traverse City, Muskegon and Cadillac.

SAN JOAQUIN VALLEY LEAGUE: J. N. Young, President, Visalia, Calif.
MEMBERS: Bakersfield, Visalia, Coalings and Tulare.

EASTERN KANSAS LEAGUE: E. M. Whitney, Secretary, Hiawatha, Kan.
MEMBERS: Seneca, Holton, Hiawatha, Horton, Sabetha and Marysville.

WASHINGTON STATE LEAGUE: W. R. McFarlane, President, Aberdeen, Wash.
MEMBERS: Aberdeen, Hoquiam, Montaseno, Raymond, Tacoma and Chehalis.

WEST VIRGINIA LEAGUE: T. S. Haymond, President, Fairmont, W. Va.
MEMBERS: Mannington, Clarksburg, Grafton, Fairmont.

PENNSYLVANIA AND WEST VIRGINIA LEAGUE: J. D. Gronninger, President, Morgantown, W. Va.

MEMBERS: Connellsville, Fairmont, Morgantown, Uniontown and Grafton. (Disbanded.)

VIRGINIA VALLEY LEAGUE: Wm. H. Barringer, President, Charleston, W. Va.

MEMBERS: Montgomery, Huntington, Charleston, Parkersburg, Pt. Pleasant, in W. Va., Ashland-Catlettsburg in Kentucky.

INDIANA-MICHIGAN LEAGUE: R. E. Proctor, President, Elkhart, Ind.

MEMBERS: Elkhart, Gary, Goshen, Ind., Niles, Berrien Springs, Benton Harbor, Mich.

CONNECTICUT ASSOCIATION: D. P. Dunn, President, Willimantic, Conn.

MEMBERS: New London, Willimantic, Norwich and Middletown, Conn. (Disbanded.)

KENTUCKY - ILLINOIS - TENNESSEE LEAGUE: C. A. Gosnell, President, Vincennes, Ind.

MEMBERS: Vincennes, Ind., Paducah, Henderson, Madisonville, Hopkinsville, Kentucky, Clarksville, Tenn.

NORTHERN ASSOCIATION: C. A. Burton, President, Jacksonville, Ill.

MEMBERS: Muscatine, Clinton, Iowa, Decatur, Joliet, Elgin, Kankakee, Freeport and Jacksonville, Ill. (Disbanded.)

SOUTHERN CALIFORNIA TROLLEY LEAGUE: J. P. McCormick, President, Los Angeles, Cal.

MEMBERS: Santa Ana, Pasadena, Redondo, The McCormicks, The Maiers, Long Beach.

NEBRASKA STATE LEAGUE: H. A. Sievers, President, Grand Island, Neb.

MEMBERS: Hastings, Red Cloud, Columbus, Superior, Seward, Kearney, Fremont and Grand Island.

MISSOURI-IOWA-NEBRASKA-KANSAS LEAGUE: T. A. Wilson, President, Clarinda, Iowa.

MEMBERS: Clarinda, Marysville, Mo., Nebraska City, Auburn, Falls City, Neb., Shenandoah, Iowa.

CENTRAL CALIFORNIA BASEBALL LEAGUE: E. H. Raymond, President, Napa, Cal.

MEMBERS: San Rafael, Napa, Vallejo, Petaluma, Point Richmond, Alameda, San Leandre, Fruitvale.

CALIFORNIA BASEBALL LEAGUE: Frank Herman, President, San Francisco, Cal.

MEMBERS: San Francisco, Sacramento, Oakland, Stockton, Fresno and San Jose. (Disbanded).

What the Player Signs.

THE tie that binds a player to his club is a uniform one in all the minor leagues, every club being required to use the same form of contract in signing its players. For the information of the fans, who would like to know just what the duties and privileges of a ball-player are, the following copy of a minor league contract is reproduced in full:

Club Presidents should Sign all Contracts.

CLASS B.

CONTRACT
APPROVED BY THE
NATIONAL ASSOCIATION OF PROFESSIONAL BASEBALL LEAGUES.

NIGHT LEAGUE OF BASEBALL CLUBS.

This Agreement, made this 29th day of February, 1912, between The Sarsaparilla Club, party of the first part, and Arthur Moonlight, part of the second part, WITNESSETH:

FIRST. Said party of the second part agrees to devote his entire time and services, as a ball player, to said party of the first part during the period of this contract.

SECOND. Said party of the second part agrees to conform to all the rulesand regulations now adopted or which may be hereafter adopted by the party of the first part, appertaining to his services aforesaid.

THIRD. Said party of the second part agrees not to render any services as a ball player, during the time of this contract, to any other person, corporation or association other than the party of the first part, without the written consent of the party of the first part so to do.

FOURTH. It is further understood and agreed between both parties to this contract that all the provisions and conditions of the National Agreement of the National Association of Professional Base Ball

Leagues be and they hereby are made a part of this contract.

In consideration of the foregoing premises the party of the first part agrees:

FIRST. To pay to the said party of the second part the sum of $40 per month, to be paid in equal semi-monthly installments, upon the first and fifteenth of every month during the championship season of the league of which first party is a member unless the ball team shall be away from home playing games, in which event the installments falling due shall be paid within the first week after the return home of the said ball team.

SECOND. Said party of the first part agrees to pay the traveling expenses, board and lodging of said party of the second part whenever said party of the second part may be traveling in the services of said party of the first part, and when not so traveling the party of the second part will pay all of his own expenses.

It is hereby mutually agreed by the parties hereto, in consideration of the premises hereinbefore set forth, that should the party of the said second part, at any time or times, or in any manner fail to comply with the covenants and agreements herein contained or any of them, or with any of the rules and regulations of the party of the first part, which are now or may hereafter from time to time be made, or should the said party of the second part at any time or times be intemperate, immoral, careless, indifferent, or conduct himself in such a manner, whether on or off the field, as to endanger or prejudice the interest of said party of the first part, or should the party of the second part become ill or otherwise unfit, from any cause whatever, or prove incompetent in the judgment of the party of the first part, then the said party of the first part hereunto shall have the right to discipline, suspend, fine or discharge the said party of the second part in such manner as to it, the said party of the first part, shall seem fit and proper, and the said party of the first part shall be the sole judge as to the sufficiency of the reason for such discipline, suspension, fine or discharge, and in case of fine imposed, it is agreed by said party of the second part that he will pay the same, or that the same may be withheld, as and for liquidated damages.

In order to enable the party of the second part to fit himself for the duties necessary under the terms of this contract, the said party of the first part may require the said party of the second part to report for practice and participate in such exhibition contests as may be arranged by said party of the first part for a period of 30 days prior to the 25th day of April, the party of the first part to pay the actual expenses of said party of the second part during said period.

It is further agreed that if the said party of the first part should desire the services of the said party of the second part for any period of time after the date mentioned for the expiration of the term mentioned herein or which may be mentioned in any renewal hereof, said first party shall have the right to the same by paying compensation to the said second party for each day at the rate of one-thirtieth (1-30) of the amount herein specified as the monthly salary of said second party.

IN WITNESS WHEREOF, the said party of the first part has caused these presents to be signed by its officer thereunto duly authorized, and the said second party has affixed his hand and seal on the day and year first above written.

By GEORGE SIPPS, President.

[SEAL]   ARTHUR MOONLIGHT.

Player Sign Here.

Outlawry.

IN the year 1903 there sprang into existence a little league that was composed of the following cities, Altoona, Harrisburg, Lebanon, Williamsport and York, Pa., Camden, N. J., and Wilmington, Del. The little league was organized on an independent basis and was named the Tri-State League. Little did the magnates, players, or the baseball public at large dream that this organization would prove a great thorn in the side of the major leagues and organized baseball in general. The late Mr. William C. Farnsworth of Harrisburg, Pa., who later presented the Farnsworth Cup, a handsome trophy for which the clubs contended annually, was the first President. Mr. Farnsworth resigned in the fall of 1904 and was succeeded by Mr. Theo. B. Creamer of Philadelphia. At the conclusion of 1905 Mr. Chas. F. Carpenter, the present occupant, took the President's chair and the real battle against organized baseball was on. Inspired by their energetic leader these Tri-State sportsmen hesitated at no expense to down their rival teams. The American and National Leagues, not saying anything about the Eastern, the American Association, and in fact all the leagues in the country, suffered from the raids of the sporting outlaws in the Keystone State. At York, George Heckert, backed by a crowd of game sportsmen, actually had a major league team in a town of less than 50,000 inhabitants. At Harrisburg, Billy Hamilton, the ex-major-leaguer, held forth with a major league club. Williamsport, the home of the "millionaires," after whom the club was named, had a team second to none in the League. The remaining clubs, as will be seen by the appended list of players, consisted of athletes who had played in the major leagues sometime in the recent past. The League was a paradise for the players. Hans Lobert, later the crack third baseman of the Cincinnati club, started in with the Johnstown club at a salary of $65.00 per month. When he left there his salary had been raised from that amount to $450.00 per month. Dave Altizer jumped from New York to Washington and back until his salary reached $850.00 per month. Joe Cantillon, afterward the manager of the Washington club, is authority for the statement that Altizer got bowlegged jumping back and forth from York to Washington. Pat Dougherty, later with the White Sox, received considerably in excess of $500.00 per month, as did a dozen other players. Very few players drew less than $1,200.00 for a four or five months' season, while others ranged from that to $3,500.00 for the season. To show what high-class clubs these little towns carried one has but to look over the following list of players, together with the clubs they later joined, or jumped from to join the Outlaws.

To the National League

NEW YORK: Wiltse, Herzog, Chief Meyers, Bull Durham, Phyle, Billy Gilbert.

CINCINNATI: Dick Egan; Dave Altizer; Hans Lobert; Billy Campbell; George Upp; Charles, infielder; Harry Arndt; Jim Wiggs; Doescher, pitcher; Chappelle, pitcher; Fred Smith; Si Pauxtis; McGilvray.

CHICAGO: Rube Kroh; Cooney, infielder; Tom Needham, catcher.

BROOKLYN: George Bell, pitcher; Eddie Lennox, third baseman; Eddie Holly, second baseman; Jack Hayden, outfielder; Chas. Malay, outfielder; Billy Keister, infielder; Fred Lewis, infielder; Al Burch, outfielder; Harry Pattee, infielder; Holmes, pitcher; McElveen, infielder; Starnagle, catcher.

PITTSBURG: Bucky Veil, pitcher; Jimmy Sebring, outfielder; Shaw, third baseman; Swacina, first baseman; Chas. Starr, infielder.

BOSTON: Bud Sharpe, first baseman; Shean, second baseman; Sam Brown, catcher; Mattern, pitcher; Moran, outfielder; Stem, first baseman; Billy Hamilton, outfielder.

PHILADELPHIA: Jacklitsch, catcher; Otto Deininger, fielder; Mike Grady, catcher; Harry Wolverton, third baseman; Martell, catcher; Baum, pitcher;

Shettler, pitcher; Crist, catcher; Hartley, outfielder; Hoch, pitcher.

ST. LOUIS: Sallee, pitcher; Stony McGlynn, pitcher; Mike Mowrey, third baseman; Joe Delehanty, outfielder; Johnnie Lush, pitcher; Dusty Rhodes, pitcher; Jack Farrell, infielder; Mike O'Neil, pitcher; Bill Steele, pitcher.

To the American League

NEW YORK: Bert Daniels, outfielder; Birdie Cree, outfielder; Ed. Foster, infielder; Manning, pitcher; Warhop, pitcher; Lewis LaRoy, pitcher; Blair, catcher; Roach, infielder.

ATHLETICS: Hoffman, infielder; Ben Hauser, first baseman; Chief Bender, pitcher; Baker, third baseman; Ed. Krause, pitcher; Morris Rath, infielder; Rube Vickers, pitcher; Hulseman, outfielder; Mike Lynch, infielder; Whalen, pitcher.

DETROIT: Bill Coughlin, third baseman; Cockhill, first baseman; Ness, first baseman; Pete Lister, first baseman; Tom Jones, outfielder; Red Killifer, infielder; Delos Drake, outfielder.

CHICAGO WHITE SOX: Pat Dougherty, outfielder; Joe Cassidy, infielder.

BOSTON: Buck Freeman, outfielder; Wolter, outfielder; Jack Hoey, outfielder; Cy Barger, pitcher; Mathews, pitcher.

CLEVELAND: Vinson, outfielder; Hinchman, outfielder; Jimmie Jackson, outfielder.

WASHINGTON: Charley Street, catcher; Dr. Reisling, pitcher; Falkenberg, pitcher; Bob Unglaub, first baseman; Otis Clymer, outfielder; Lelivelt, pitcher; Lefty George, pitcher; Jack Crooks, first baseman.

From the foregoing list of players one might well wonder how towns of this size could support these major league teams. All of these cities boasted of Angels, and were game from first to last. At Altoona Rudy Bockel forsook a paying contracting business for the diamond and went the limit in securing a winning team. Bockel started the season with six second basemen, Tim Flood, Eddy Holly, Fred Raymer, Eddie Lennox, Billy Lauterborn and Jack Farrell; any one of these men was good enough for any major league club. Lauterborn was so disgusted at beholding so many second basemen that he jumped back to Syracuse, N. Y., where he came from stating that the Tri-State League was the "dag-gone'dst League he had ever been in. Why, they got so many second-sackers that I did not get a chance to even warm up."

As pitchers, Bockel had: George Bell, now with the Brooklyn club; Jim Wiggs, Chas. Baum, whom Philadelphia later secured; Doescher, later with Cincinnati, also Chappelle who joined the same club. Behind the bat he had Starnagle, still with Brooklyn, and Tommy Needham, now with the Cubs. Burch, now with Brooklyn; Bates, recently traded to Cincinnati; and Otto Deininger, later with Philadelphia, constituted the Altoona outfield. This aggregation of stars cost Bockel $6,500.00 the first month of the season. In his generosity he distributed his surplus second basemen among his rival clubs throughout the League. Talk about game sportsmen, Bockel had them all tied down. His losses reached the

M. H. SEXTON
President of the National Association

$25,000 mark the two seasons he was in the game in his vain effort to land the pennant for his home town—Altoona.

Williamsport also spared no expense in landing the best talent available. With Bob Unglaub, now with Washington, Johnnie Lush, with St. Louis, Jimmie Sebring, later with Pittsburg and Cincinnati, Cockhill of Detroit, it had its surplus of stars and seemed able to land the pennant at will. Every club in the League had an abundance of star players.

There were many ludicrous incidents that the players pulled off on the long-suffering magnates. One of the pet schemes they would practice was to wire one another from town to town stating that the sender was an agent from some major league club and would be pleased to meet the receiver at some distant town. The player would rush immediately to the club directors who would hurriedly hold a meeting and the scheming players would invariably be granted an increase in salary. The League itself would send out its scouts to neighboring leagues, and these poor fellows surely had their troubles. I remember one in particular, Alec Pearson, who came to Scranton and Wilkesbarre to gather in the best men of those two clubs. The coal miners in these two towns were not long in discovering Pearson's errand, and the latter broke all records in that part of the country getting out of town—minus his prey.

The losses of these game sportsmen ran up into the hundreds of thousands. When the angels would temporarily tire of their constant losses, the citizens of the game little towns would set aside a benefit day. Every patron of the game was obliged to put up one dollar on this day, and in this manner quite large sums were collected which would tide the club over its financial straits for a few weeks. This paradise for the ball players, however, could not last forever. By their exorbitant demands and mismanagement, they beat themselves, for in January, 1907, under the superb leadership of its President, Charles F. Carpenter, the League decided to apply for membership in the National Association of Minor Leagues. The application was rewarded with the territory of the cities of Wilmington, Del., and Trenton, N. J. Quite a number of high-class players who were still the property of the former outlaws were disposed of, the League thereby realizing the neat sum of $28,450. Outlawry, of course, after the League's admission to the National Association, was abandoned, owing to the enforcement of penalties, by the officials of organized ball, against the deserters from the ranks, and the consequent inability to secure players for 1907. When a League of this size undertakes to make warfare against not only the National and American Leagues, but thirty other Leagues banded together, it is going against tremendous odds, with annihilation only a question of time. The fact that it existed as long as it did, can be attributed to a number of good game backers, chief among whom I may mention Chas. Bockel of Altoona; Bill Tunis of Harrisburg; Frank Bowman and Thos. Gray of Williamsport; George K. Kline and Ollie Blough of Johnstown; John H. Myers, C. Trout and Col. Perrine of Trenton, N. J. It may be added that this bunch of enthusiasts will be hard to duplicate. Where will you find another crowd that is in the game solely for the pleasure they derive from it, without regard to expense?

Browning's Last Can.

IN 1892 I was a member of the Allentown club of the Pennsylvania State League. Marty Swift, a whole-souled Irishman, who was the possessor of a rich brogue, was the manager of the Scranton club, and on his team were Eddie Sales and Jerry McCormick. The former occasionally indulged in the flowing bowl, notwithstanding which fact he was a powerful batsman. "I see by the morning papers," said Swift to McCormick one day, "that Eddie Sales leads the League by forty p'ints." "Arrah, go on," replied McCormick, "the way Eddie has been biting them off lately, he must lead the League by at least forty quarts." Two years later in Allentown they had a great crowd of old-timers. The team was led by the late Mike Kelly and financed by the well-known street car magnate, Al Johnson, of Cleveland, Ohio. Although Allentown boasted of less than 50,000 inhabitants, the same salaries were paid as in the major league. Kelly and Big Jack Milligan were the catchers, Mark Baldwin, Kilroy and Red Donahue, later with Cleveland, pitchers; Ted Larkin, first base; Sam Wise, second base; Sweeney, shortstop; Joe Mulvey, third base; George Wood, left field; the noted Pete Browning, center field, and Costello, right field. All of these men with the exception of Costello and Sweeney were direct from the National League and were paid enormous salaries. Pete Browning in his day was one of the most powerful of batsmen, but a notorious record-player. No matter how badly the club was beaten, Browning was happy when he had a brace of hits. When asked, "What's the score, Pete?" he would reply, "Oh, I only got four today, a home-run, a triple and two singles." Browning lost his job with Kelly in a rather ludicrous manner. With the score a tie in the ninth inning, our leftfielder, Jack Wolters, hit a ball to left center into a small pool of water that had accumulated from a rainstorm that morning. Browning gave chase to the ball. The hit might have been good for two bases even had Browning recovered the ball out of the pool, but he was evidently afraid to get his trilbies wet, for he ran around the pool like a great big long turkey. By the time the ball was dragged out of the water by one of Browning's teammates, Wolters had crossed the plate with the winning run. Kelly was furious. He landed a couple of uppercuts on Browning's mustache and released him on the spot. Poor Pete played no more baseball after that. He died a few years later.

A Trio of Stars.

IN my twenty years' experience in the minor leagues it has been my pleasure to witness the debut of three of the greatest stars the game has ever produced. Away back in 1890 I was trying to play on one of the many amateur teams in my native city of

Cincinnati. Ren Mulford, the well-known baseball authority of the Queen City, picked me off the lots, after I had tramped his back stairs importuning him to get me a position with some minor league until the janitor threatened me with bodily harm. Mr. Mulford, much to my delight, sent me to Canton, Ohio, then a member of the Ohio League. I lost no time starting out for Canton. Arriving there I accosted a stranger at the depot, inquiring of him if he knew at what hotel the players were stopping. He replied that he was looking for the same information. Together we started on our hunt for the hotel, which we found in a short time. I well remember our arrival there. The players evidently did not like my companion's makeup, for loud was the laughter and irritating the jibes that were hurled our way. The laughter and jibes, however, ceased the instant my companion stepped on the field for practice the next day. The way he would hurl that ball past the ambitious batsman was a caution. On the next Sunday they put him into the box against some Pennsylvania League club that had been making a tour of our League, playing exhibition games. Eighteen of the visitors went out on strikes. The kidding match was now turned into an admiration society. Our League disbanded early in August, and I went back to the lots in my native town. Tom Loftus was then at the head of the Cincinnati club. Not long after my arrival home I met my sponsor in professional ball—Mr. Mulford. Ever ready to be of assistance to help strengthen the club that represented his native town, he asked me:—"Eddie, are there any players up in that League that we could use here in Cincinnati?" "Yes," I replied, "there is a big pitcher we had at Canton who is good enough for any club." With this information, Mr. Mulford rushed to the Cincinnati management, but they failed to act, and a few days after this incident my companion pitched his first game in major league circles, wearing a Cleveland uniform, against Anson's Chicago club, giving them a measly three hits. He was none other than the world-famous Denton T. Young, whose record will never be equaled.

While owner of the Charleston club, of the South Atlantic League, my team was frequently scheduled at Augusta, Ga. On this club was a youngster who attracted my attention in a rather queer way. He was continually running. He would run up to bat, run back to the bench, run in and out from his position. He was running all the time. I never saw a young lad so full of life and enthusiasm over the game. "Lock the gates," the bleachers would yell. The instant he reached a base he was gone on to the next one, a veritable whirlwind. He was so fast that he was not obliged to even slide. At the bat, by natural instinct he took advantage of his great speed and on numerous occasions bunted the ball and easily reached the coveted base. All that winter I tried to get him, with no success. In the following spring the Detroit club trained at Augusta under the management of Wm. Armour. When the team left for the North, they left a young pitcher with the Augusta club by the name of Eddie Cicotte for further development. Our season opened in due time and I again opened negotiations for this speed demon and thought at last that I was to be successful in landing him.

HUMOR AMONG THE MINORS

We were playing Augusta and it was a hard battle all the way through. The score was 2 to 0 in favor of Augusta in the last inning with two of my men on the bases and Sid. Smith, now with Cleveland, at the bat. Smith hit a terrific line drive to short center field. In came the speedy one, in his very daring way tried to intercept the ball and, falling short, the ball took a nasty bound and rolled to the fence. My two runners and Smith scored, winning the game for Charleston. Mr. Carter, the president of the club, met me as we were leaving the grounds and was furious over the loss of the game. "Take him, Ash, you can have him as a gift," he said. "All right," I replied, "will see you later." I saw Mr. Carter later, after he had cooled down somewhat. "I'll take the young fellow with me," I said to Pres. Carter. "You will, if you pay me what it cost me to carry him this spring," he replied. "All right, what did he cost you?" I asked. "Give me $25.00 and I will send him over to you in Charleston by Monday." I gave Pres. Carter my check with instructions to send my man over to me on the first train. I awaited his coming on Monday with much anxiety, but no speedy youngster showed up. The next day I received a letter from Pres. Carter calling the deal off. He had made previous arrangements with the Detroit club whereby that club was to have first selection of all the Augusta players for the privilege of using pitcher Cicotte. The speed demon was none other than the now famous Ty. Cobb, and do you wonder I get a severe pain in the head when I think how close I once came to buying a—well, say—$25,000 asset for a measly $25.00?

HUMOR AMONG THE MINORS

In the year 1900, after ten years of playing in various small leagues, the Virginia League magnates very generously handed to me gratis the Hampton franchise of the Virginia League. I arrived at Hampton in due time, and looked over the field. The outlook was not brilliant, so I declined to invest my little savings in a proposition that gave such small promise. However, the League, rather than make those long railroad jumps to Lynchburg and Roanoke, decided to finance my club at Hampton. The League was composed of Richmond, Petersburg, Norfolk, Portsmouth, Newport News and Hampton. The Norfolk club had on their team that year a big strapping stripling of a youngster. This lad's position was in the pitcher's box. The way he would hurl the ball across the plate was a caution. This youth was indefatigable. He was always the first player out at the grounds for morning practice, working on his control, thus perfecting himself in his chosen profession. A player showing such inclinations cannot help but succeed. Here, indeed was a diamond in the rough, showing by his every action on the field that he was a coming star. I lost no time in writing to Mr. Charles W. Murphy, now President of the Cubs, and requesting him to inform the Cincinnati club of this husky and willing youngster down in Norfolk. I failed to hear from Mr. Murphy and the Cincinnati club lost a player who by his phenomenal pitching saved his entire league from financial ruin and possible disruption at the hands of its rival, the American League. The ambitious, ever-willing, hustling youth was none other than Christy Mathewson.

Killed the Goose that Laid the Golden Egg.

IN 1901 I owned the Newport News-Hampton club in the Virginia League. We went along finely until the Fourth of July. After that it was a hard struggle and salary days were few and far between. Virginia rooters are not unlike all Dixie fans, the most enthusiastic and loyal supporters in the land. When a player makes a phenomenal catch or a timely hit, his act is rewarded with a shower of silver from the grandstand and bleachers. We were playing Richmond one day and it was a fierce battle and went into extra innings. Playing first base for me was Al Weddige, who was considered one of the heaviest hitters in minor league balldom. In the twelfth inning of that contest, in going to bat Weddige remarked to me, "Ash, it's all over with the game now. I'll put the ball over the fence." Sure enough, Weddige placed a beauty over the left field fence. Did you ever see a Dixie audience? Well, you ought to have seen this one. The crowd fairly went wild. Dollars, halves, quarters, dimes and nickels came pouring out of the stand and bleachers onto the field. It was a regular silver shower. Weddige came tearing around the bases with his face all lit up in smiles. When he arrived close to third base he gazed toward the stand, his jaw dropped, and instead of keeping on to third base and then to the plate, he rushed pell mell through the diamond yelling like mad, for there were the rest of my players picking up the silver like a chicken eating corn. When the boys got through picking up the money there was very little left for Weddige, who was wild. Both the boys and Weddige could hardly be blamed, for that was the first money they had seen that month. Now for the sequel; Weddige, in rushing through the diamond after his mad rush for the money, had not touched third base and of course the umpire had declared him out for his failure to touch the bag. Instantly there was a commotion. Weddige, a few moments before, was a hero, but now a dub, a load of hay, etc. The game finally went on. Tannehill, now with the White Sox, but then playing short stop for Richmond, put the ball over the fence for a home run. He touched all the bases, and there were no more silver showers.

A Lengthy Argument.

IN 1902 I transferred operations from the Virginia-League, taking the management of the Charlotte, N. C., in the North Carolina League. I well remember a trio of celebrities this little League developed. George Suggs, now the winning pitcher of the Cincinnati club, Arthur Devlin, for years the star third baseman of the New York Giants, and the late Jimmie Sebring. Poor Jimmie was extremely ambitious, although it was his first season out. He evidently heard that I was acting as agent for a certain major league club. "Take me, Ash," said Jimmie, "I am certain I will fill the bill." When I told him his extreme youth was against him, he said, "Never mind, Ash, I'll be up among the big fellows at no distant date." Poor Sebring's prediction was verified even sooner than he expected, for that fall some major league club picked him up. His work in Cincinnati and Pittsburg is still remembered with keen pleasure by the fans of those cities. My Charlotte club that season made a record for winning consecutive games, not only winning the pennant, hands down, but taking twenty-five consecutive games. This feat broke up my little league, and in August of that year I accepted the management of the Shreveport, La., club of the Southern League. Con Strouthers had the Chattanooga club that year and in a game against my club pulled off a laughable one on a little umpire named Stanton. This poor chap was away off in his work and argument after argument arose. Finally Stanton was in the middle of the diamond with both teams hauling and jerking him around. Strouthers was fairly frothing at the mouth in his frenzy. Finally he shouted to his lieutenant, Ike Durrett, "Here, Ike! hold the argument until I get a drink of water."

The same year Strouthers' club was up in the race and had visions of the pennant. Calling his men together for a final talk, Strouthers said, "Boys, keep on fighting. Think of all the glories and honor that will be bestowed on us should we land the championship." His lieutenant nearly broke up the meeting by interrupting Strouthers. "Pennant bosh!" exclaimed Durrett; "why, if we would win the pennant in this town, the niggers would come out some night and steal it, if not, the knockers would." Chattanooga has changed mightily since that time, and is now one of the best baseball cities in the South.

Riding Out on a Rail.

A LITTLE trick that a thoughtless left fielder of mine tried to pull off on the home team at Wilmington, N. C., in 1902, gave me a bad afternoon at that hustling town. I was at the head of the Charlotte, N. C., club, and we were in the midst of a long winning streak, that ended in my team winning twenty-five consecutive games. We were playing Wilmington that day and the game was very one-sided in our favor. I retired early during the game and directed my club from the bench. As my team was winning with ease the crowd was in anything but a good humor, and they were joshing and guying us from the instant we went ahead of them in the game. It was about the fifth inning that the trouble started. My left fielder, a foxy sort of a chap, ever ready to pull off a trick that would benefit his club, led not only himself but the entire club and myself into the fracas. He always had an old practice ball concealed on his person. In the event that the opportunity presented itself for him to pull off a trick of some sort, he would endeavor to put the old ball into play. One of the Wilmington batsmen hit a terrific drive out into his territory. The grass was rather high, but the ball was seen to roll under the fence outside of the grounds. My left fielder ran in pursuit of the ball until he was close to the fence, when he stooped and picked a ball out of the grass and relayed it to second base, where the batsman was put out. "Out," yelled the umpire. I guess everybody on the grounds thought alike except the umpire. Although we were so far ahead in the game that chances of the home team overtaking us seemed impossible, the people swarmed out on the field. When the umpire saw them coming he waved them back, yelling, "The batter is safe," pointing to a child who had recovered the original ball and was running toward the umpire with it. The crowd, however, was now on the field and had to wreak vengeance on somebody, so they started after my tricky left fielder. The leaders of the crowd seized him and I ran into the mob to protect him. One of the crowd was so excited that he displayed a drawn revolver. I had a big pitcher, Buck Brand, who with the utmost calmness took the weapon away from the fellow, and with a healthy kick sent him on his way. The police did not seem anxious to assist us, in fact, they were as hostile as any one in the mob. However, at this stage the sheriff reached the scene and the mob fell back in short order. The sheriff said to me, "Come on, Ash." I accompanied him, while the police with my left fielder followed amid loud cries of "Ride 'em out of town on a rail," from the countrymen. One look from the sheriff and the crowd again fell back. In the meantime we had arrived at the stand, and the sheriff, espying the umpire, asked him, "Which one of these fellows do you want out of here?" The lot fell to my left fielder, who was ejected from the grounds.

The game then went on and we added insult to injury, for we piled up run after run. This only added fuel to the flames. The rail-riders could be heard muttering dire things as to what they would do to us after the game. At last the game was over and we wended our way to the bus, and, notwithstanding that the police accompanied us on our ride back to our hostelry we were the recipients of a shower of mud and rocks at the hands of the mob. Arriving at the hotel we were congratulating ourselves that the trouble was at its end, but we were mistaken. When we reached the depot our trouble commenced again. The mob wanted our left fielder. He had anticipated trouble and had concealed himself on the train. "Bring him out here, Ash," they yelled; "if you don't we'll give you the ride." I laughed at this and tried to look at the threat as a joke, when they seized me, intending to give me the rail-ride. But they only grabbed me, that's all. A big mouthy leader who had a strong hold on me went down as if the building had fallen on him. Down went another and another. The big pitcher Brand had got to working again and the would-be riders dropped like ten-pins. The only ones injured were the riders, who went down the street in record time.

In justice to the citizens of Wilmington, they were profuse in their apologies to me personally and to my players, denouncing the action of the riders as that of rowdies and hoodlums of the worst type. While the act of my tricky left fielder was doubtless open for censure, there might have been serious trouble but for the courageous action of the big fellow Brand. As for my left fielder he had the scare of his life, and thereafter would not even look at a ball, unless it was in the game.

It was at Macon, Ga., I got mine one fine day in 1904. We were playing Macon and at about the fifth inning, the attendance being small, I went into the box office to settle for the day's receipts. I was in playing uniform and put my part of the receipts into my hip pocket. In leaving the grounds, as is usual after a game, everybody rushed for the street cars in the desire to get a seat. We were all in the crowd when I felt a short pull at my trousers pocket where I had the money. Quick as a flash I turned and seized the hand that was after the money. It was a small urchin, and in his struggles to get away I accidentally stepped on his foot with my spiked shoe. Instantly there was an uproar. The lad claimed I had intentionally spiked him, and the crowd, not being aware of the urchin's hand in my pocket, became quite indignant, and loud were their threats to make a complaint against me in court. Arriving at the hotel we were preparing to leave Macon for Savannah, when Billy Smith, who was then manager of the Macon club, rushed into my room, saying, "Look at that mob down there, Ash! For Heaven's sake come quick into my room and hide." I was no more than in Smith's room, when in came two big policemen. "Where is Ash?" asked one of them, named O'Rourke, with whom I had been friends for ten years. "Don't know. He's around the building somewhere," I replied. With a repressed smile he left Smith's room. The crowd in the meantime was blocking the entrance to the hotel, and as soon as the police left, in came a lot of constables, the urchin's guardian having entered charges against me with some Justice of the Peace. I heard that a bunch of constables would search the building for me. I left Smith's room and wandered down to the kitchen of the hotel. "Are you the boy they're after?" asked a sweet, pleasant voice. "Yes, yes," I replied. "Here, my boy, put this on, here, put this on, quick," handing me a white jacket and cap, the uniform of the cook. I put it on and had no more than done so, when in came the country sleuths. They even looked in the coal bin for me. Much to my relief they left the kitchen. I tried to thank my benefactress, who happened to be our landlord's venerable mother, but it was no use. All this time I wanted to give myself up to the police, for it was the mob and not the police I feared. Finally the landlord and three or four gentlemen entered the kitchen. One old fellow seized my hands, heartily shaking them. "We saw it all, we saw it all. Come on with us, Mr. Ashenback. No harm shall befall you." We left the hotel by a rear entrance and they led me to the police headquarters. Arriving there, they sent for the boy who claimed I had attacked him with my spiked shoes. He came in due time with his guardian, who wanted to murder me. However, the Chief of Police knew the little fellow, who had just been released from a reformatory for thievery. My friends, who had seen the entire incident from a car seat, added to this their explanation and I was released with ample apologies from the lad's guardian. The newspapers had a full account of the affair the next morning completely vindicating me. The lad, I was informed, was sent back to the Reform School. The funny part of this incident that looked so serious and caused me so much trouble, was the size of my roll of money which was so large that, when the urchin reached down into my pocket, it swelled his hand out of all proportion and he could not get his little fist out of my pocket.

JOHN H. FARRELL
Secretary of the National Association

My club left Macon shortly after the game on an accommodation train that would make all stops. The Macon police, evidently thinking that I would get on the train at some small station near Macon, had sent two officers on the train with my club. Again the practical joker was at work, for the boys told me that at every station where some person would get on, the boys would look out of the car window and yell at the approaching passenger, "Look out, Ash!" The passenger would look up at them in a bewildered manner as he entered the car, The boys would yell, "Hide, Ash, hide! The cops are here." The police would seize the bewildered countryman and try to make him admit that he was Ashenback. The boys kept this up until the police left the train.

Dear Old Dixie.

ALTHOUGH a Yankee by birth, I shall never forget the dear old rooters who dwell below the Mason and Dixie Line. Neither will I forget some of Dixie's sons, to many of whom I gave employment during my career in the Southland. My first visit to the south was in the year 1894, when I played with Ted Sullivan's Atlanta, Ga., club of the Southern League. The following year I went with Sullivan to Dallas, Texas. 1897 also found me in Texas. 1900, 1901, 1902, 1904-1905 found me still in Dixieland. Bless the old boys that I signed from that southern country! They were the soul of honor, and could be depended on at all times. They have a queer, lovable dialect, that one cannot help but enjoy. On my southern teams were Champ Osteen, afterwards with St. Louis; Arthur Brouthers, a protege of mine, who was later picked up by Connie Mack; Eddie Persons, a left-handed pitcher; Ernie Murray; Sidney Smith, who hails from one of South Carolina's foremost families; Bob Chappelle, later with Cincinnati; Hogan Yancey, later in the Eastern League, and Doc Childs, who has been mentioned elsewhere in this book. It was quite a long time before I acquired or even could understand their dialect. Childs and Smith constituted a battery for me, and in their anxiety to please me would have a "chewing match" every game they worked. Childs, an extremely powerful fellow, was often more or less wild, and I always cautioned his catcher, Smith, to let him take plenty of time in his delivery, so that he would not give so many bases on balls. The very minute Childs would have two balls on the batsman, and showed any inclination to become wild, Smith would take the ball and walk out to the box and say: "Look 'ee yeah, Doc, unbotton yoh collah, there is somethin' the matter with yoh neck." "Gimme de ball, Sidney," Childs would come back; "don't yoh-all see Mr. Eddie peeping out yere at us?" "I doan' care foh Mr. Eddie or nobody. I know what yoh-all want to do. Yoh-all want to give a base on balls."

On one occasion, some of the boys had been playing jokes on Smith in the club-house. He was about to assault one of the players, and I stepped up to them to prevent possible trouble, when Murray, who had been listening in a quiet manner to the controversy said, "Oh, pshaw, Mr. Eddie, let Sidney be. He cain't fight. He only make believe."

Pitcher Childs occasionally had afflictions of stomach trouble. One day he came to me and said, "Mr. Eddie, I cain't pitch today. I'm got de bellyache." I asked him to go in and pitch anyhow, and do the best he could, as I was short of pitchers. He went in and shut out his club. The next time he had "bellyache," Smith loudly implored me to put Childs in the box again. Would you believe it, he shut his club out without a hit or a run? The boys gradually drifted north, I taking Murray, Graham, Chappelle, Yancey and Persons with me to Scranton. That these boys possessed ability was shown conclusively when my Scranton club won the pennant hands down in the New York League.

The Southern lads put me into an awful tight hole at Scranton one day. We were scheduled for an exhibition game with a crack colored club. One and all to a man they refused to play against the colored club, and with the loss of these men my club was wofully weakened and we were rather easy marks for our dusky brethren. That night the boys seemed rather crestfallen, and the next day they came in a body to me saying, "Look yeah, Mr. Eddie, we been kind 'shamed of the boys the way them col'ed folks pounced on ouah club yestehday, and we are askin' if we-all cain't sneak in there today and help bust them niggahs." I readily gave my consent and what they did to the colored cracks was a caution.

Three of the boys at Albany, N. Y., came very near getting into serious trouble at an opera house one night. They had been to the show and everything went off all right until the orchestra struck up "Dixie," when up went a yell from this trio that shook the building. They seemed very much put out over the lack of enthusiasm which the audience showed, and very much more crestfallen when the usher politely but firmly asked them to leave the theatre.

A Bonehead Play.

HARRY WOLVERTON, who had great success in winning pennants in the Tri-State League, once had as one of his outfielders Warren Miller, the youngster who now belongs to Washington. Miller was caught napping off first base one day, and of course Wolverton told him "something" good and plenty. The very next day Miller was caught napping off second base. "What in the world are you doing out there on that base, standing there as if in a trance? What in the blazes are you thinking of?" yelled Harry. "Well, I'll tell you what I was thinking of, Mr. Wolverton. I was thinking of that call you gave me yesterday," said Miller. Dense silence.

Caught with the Goods.

WHEN I owned the Charleston club it was always my delight to have a Sunday game scheduled at Jacksonville, Fla., as it meant a large crowd for me. We had a big day down there one Sunday in 1904, the crowd flowing all over the field. We began hitting all of the Jacksonville pitchers, and finally Manager Kelly of the Jacksonville club rushed out to the gate and pulled off a pitcher whom he had stationed there to take tickets. The youngster came into the game plainly embarrassed. Still he went fine until, in endeavoring to field a bunt, he in some manner spiked himself. His stocking was ripped up the leg, and there was a stream of nickels, dimes and other coin sprinkled all over the diamond, which this youngster had appropriated on the gate. Doubtless the large audience was wondering what the players were picking up during the remainder of the game. The youngster was taken in tow by the management, made to disgorge. and was released on the spot.

A Quartette of Stars.

IN the year 1903 I transferred my operations from Dixieland to the New England League, assuming the management of the Nashua, N. H., club. The club was owned by a wealthy citizen of the small New Hampshire town, a prospective Governor of the State, who was that fall to enter upon his campaign for gubernatorial honors. I arrived in Nashua and was told to go ahead and spare no expense in securing a winning team, thereby giving the "Governor" all the advertisement possible. I secured my club and we were winners from the start. The mileage in the New England League is very small, in fact, all the travel is done by trolley, the towns being so closely situated. This only added to the rivalry of the games. I had a fair nucleus of a club when I took charge, and to these men I added Tim Jordan, afterward the famous first baseman of the Brooklyn club, Tommy Dowd, the well-known ex-National League player and now a minor league manager, and George Suggs, now a successful pitcher with the Cincinnati club. While my team was winning plenty of games the impetuous "Governor" was not satisfied. "Strengthen the team," he told me. To satisfy him, I journeyed on to Boston. The American League club had at that time a surplus of players, so I tried to get Jimmie Collins to let me have Nick Altrock, later a winning pitcher for the White Sox. I failed in my mission, but was informed by a friend that I could secure a great young catcher. After thanking my informant as to this catcher's whereabouts, I sailed from Portland, Me., for St. Johns, N. B., and fortunately on my arrival there found a game in progress. I lost no time in getting out to the grounds and one look at my man was satisfactory to me. He was a long, stringy, wiry-looking chap, and the way he hit the ball and threw to bases was a caution. I approached him after the game and introduced myself, stating I was there to do business with him. "My name is John McLean," he said. "They call me Long Larry down around Boston. Just get me out of this herring-eating country, and I'll catch for you for nothing."

I finally signed McLean for $125.00 per month. Tim Jordan and Suggs received the same amount.

Notwithstanding the "Governor's" extravagant methods in securing new players, it was amusing to note the economical schemes used in traveling. The club would leave for the city where it was scheduled and after the game would return to the home town. That year the players were handed their allowance for the evening meal. This magnificent amount was twenty-five cents. The players would make a mad rush for the nearest restaurant where "brown bread and lozenges" (beans) predominated. Can you imagine me handing over twenty-five cents to this quartette, Dowd, Jordan, Suggs and McLean, at this day? Dowd, who always was a Beau Brummel, laughingly told me to keep the twenty-five cents and get my shoes shined.

With McLean in my line-up, my team was even stronger. I remember well his debut at Manchester, N. H. At the bat he had four two-base hits out of four times up, and it was only the short fence that prevented the hits from being good for the circuit. The season progressed and my club was going fine. The "Governor" now promised each man a handsome bonus in event we won the pennant. The season had but three weeks to go, when I was handed a well-earned indefinite suspension by Pres. Tim Murnane for umpire-baiting. I was not even allowed my place on the bench. "When the cat is away, the mice will play," applied to this case, for my team lacked a pilot on the field and we went down to defeat with alarming regularity. As a result the championship drifted down to the very last game of the season, when my club, suffering from their long fight, went down to decisive defeat at the hands of Fred Lake's Lowell club. The "Governor" however, was a good game sport. He paid all the players the promised bonus though they had not won the pennant. The franchise that he took as a plaything and advertisement really proved a paying one. The only error the "Governor" made all that season was when he suggested that I have the players wear crash uniforms and collars and ties on Saturdays and holidays.

Coaching From Extremes.

I GUESS I was some umpire-baiter during my early managerial career. One facetious New England League sporting writer once stated in his sheet that I was removed from the game about every time the clock struck. Col. Wm. McCullom, the eminent President of the Susquehanna League in Pennsylvania, and sporting editor of a Wilkesbarre paper, during my career in the New York State League, daily published a percentage column giving my average in being removed from the game. There is nothing in this umpire-baiting. After fighting them for years, I have come to the conclusion that it's an even break all around. The arbitrator is not out to rob any one. He is trying as hard as you are; what to your mind he may appear to take away from you today, will come back to you at some future day. That has been my experience. I have had some fun with the umps in the old days. During my career in the New England League we had a red hot race for the pennant, and the arbitrator would quite frequently invite me to "lam it out of the park." We were playing at Haverhill, Mass., one day. Elsewhere in this volume is told of the economical habits we pursued in that League. Instead of dressing at the hotel the players were obliged to dress at some place adjoining the ball grounds, so that they could make the necessary connections in time to get back to their home town. In Haverhill a house close to the grounds was secured by me. The building directly overlooked the grounds, being less than a hundred feet from the playing field. The players' dressing rooms were located on the top floor of the building. The windows of the rooms led to a small roof on which an ideal view of the game could be had. I got mine from the umpire one afternoon, was put out of the game and then finally out of the grounds. In disgust I left the park and hied myself to the dressing room. Arriving there, I heard an uproar on the grounds, and rushing to the roof, found our landlady, from whom we rented the dressing rooms, wildly gesticulating and threatening the umpire from her position on the roof. The umpire had just put my catcher, Larry McLean, out of the game, arousing the ire of the worthy lady. In a minute I was out on the roof beside the worthy Celt, who tried so hard to protect her tenants, and before I knew it we were both coaching my club on. The crowd went wild, evidently appreciating the old Irish lady's sincerity in her efforts. The game was over and the players came in to dress, and with them the umpire, who also dressed at the place. He appeared in due time, but, out into the street went his clothes, the landlady wildly yelling that no "thieving empire" could even take his hat off in her residence. I received a gentle reminder of this little episode from Pres. Murnane in the shape of a $10.00 fine for being removed from the game, and an additional $5.00 as a hint to find a more appropriate place to coach my men from than a roof.

Another time at Harrisburg, Pa., Tom Walker put me out of the game and finally out of the park, also. I was obstinate and refused to go. He called an officer and as he approached me I seized a bicycle that happened to be there, mounted it and pedaled slowly away from the country policeman. To my surprise he gave pursuit, and I led him on. I soon had him winded, and kept on with the bicycle, doing circus stunts to the delight of the fans. I was coming down a steep grade with both legs on the handle bars, bowing to imaginary applause, when, crash, I went into the yap policeman who had taken a short cut to intercept me. Down we both went, amid the laughter of the crowd. I went out peaceably with the officer, while the bleachers yelled for me to put the copper out.

Flirtation with Dame Fortune.

IN 1904 I migrated to Charleston, S. C. With Jack Grim, Wm. A. (Billy) Smith, Chas. Boyer and Con Strouthers we organized the snug little South Atlantic League, with clubs at Charleston, Columbia, Macon, Jacksonville, Savannah and Augusta, Ga. After much hard labor we launched this little league, meeting with much opposition from the clannish citizens who were opposed to alien ownership. I took the Charleston franchise, and as I was not blessed with an abundance of the wherewithal to finance the club, I tried hard to organize a stock company. In this I failed, so I determined to go ahead with the club to the best of my ability. The street car company of Charleston had sufficient confidence in my ability to build me a ball grounds that cost considerably over the $10,000 mark. With the park not fully completed and still in course of erection, I sold advertising rates on the fence to the merchants of Charleston. To an enterprising merchant I sold the refreshment privilege. Then I went to work and secured advertisements for the scorecard. All this time I was signing up my club, and with the income from those privileges I finally brought on my players. I had the good fortune to book several major league clubs immediately after the arrival of my players and the income from these games, together with the neat sum secured from the advertising and refreshment privileges, netted me quite a fair roll to go ahead on. I was now a full-fledged magnate. Those fans who wanted season tickets, were accommodated at a good price. Of these many were disposed of, and a venture that was backed by nothing but a little nerve and hard, consistent work bid fair to prove a large success.

The championship season finally opened. On such short notice I had really gathered a very good team, mostly composed of southern college players. These collegians added to my prestige socially, and my attendance far exceeded expectations. The people I had tried to interest in my venture were now commencing to take notice, and several flattering offers were made me, which I, of course, sensibly refused. The season went on with my club playing finely and drawing immense crowds. My venture was a gold mine and the season closed with my profits well up in the five figures. All that winter the "Wolves" had been at work on the alien owners of our little league. Jack Grim, who owned the Columbia franchise, was the first one of the League fathers to be compelled to drop out. Con Strouthers followed at Augusta. It was not all roses with me upon my arrival at Charleston. My perpetual lease on the ground was worthless to me on some technicality, I was informed. The City Council was agitating the licensing of every club that visited Charleston. The newspapers charged me exorbitant advertising rates. Numerous other obstacles were thrown in my way, and at last I was forced to dispose of my holdings, which I did at a very good profit. The day of alien ownership is past, and it gives me pleasure to state that I disposed of my holdings in the nick of time, as my persecutors soon ran the game into the ground. I always will be grateful for the little Goddess of Fortune that sent me on my way to Charleston and my penniless investment that turned out so profitably.

A Phenomenal Catcher.

TO the average enthusiast it would appear that none but a man possessed of the utmost steadiness and nerve could fill the bill behind the bat. In 1902 and 1904 I had a catcher who was a positive marvel taken from a physical standpoint. This young man came to me highly recommended by Bill Donovan, the well-known pitcher of the Detroit club, and Bill's recommendations were more than fulfilled. When the young catcher reported to me I could hardly believe my eyes. The poor fellow was afflicted with St. Vitus' dance of the most malignant type. Owing to his affliction we will call this young man Duffy. His ailment was of such a nature that he could hardly keep quiet. Night and day he would keep up a constant barking. When behind the bat, he would constantly coach his pitcher. "Whoa, whoa, steady, my boy," he would shout, at the same time going throughout all sorts of jerks and nervous moves. When the ball was pitched it was his good fortune or gift to receive the ball in a most steady manner. He was sure on high foul balls, and joshingly styled himself "King Duff, Death to the High Flies." So far as ability was concerned he surely was accurate on everything that came his way behind the bat. It was a perfect picture to see him throw to bases, and every second he was behind the bat his active brain was working, for the way he was catching ambitious baserunners off the bases showed conclusively that he was possessed of an active baseball mind. At the bat, many a pitcher would hesitate to deliver the ball to Duffy owing to his affliction. Their fears, however, were in vain, for Duffy was an artist with the willow. While not a hard hitter he took advantage of his phenomenal speed and beat out many an infield hit. I always smile when I remember what he pulled off on me in a game between my Shreveport club and Chattanooga. Duffy was experiencing quite a prolonged hitting slump and was worrying and fretting over his bad fortune at the bat. "If I ever get a base hit," he said to the players, "I'll never stop running." Sure enough in this game at Chattanooga, with the bases full, Duffy hit a short Texas Leaguer into the outfield. He set sail for first base and never stopped, rushing all the runners in ahead of him, for the Chattanooga players had heard of his threat in the event he made a hit and applied all their efforts to head off Duffy in his mad and eccentric dash around the bases. They finally landed him at the plate. I did not reprimand him for his eccentric dash, for his single would have driven in only two runs but for his wild base running.

A ludicrous, yet pathetic incident took place on the same trip at Nashville. They had a groundkeeper there by the name of McGuire, who was afflicted with the same ailment Duffy had, and at the grounds one afternoon, Duffy was seen to be watching McGuire in his nervous gyrations and movements. "Is that fellow mocking me?" he observed. "If he is, I'll go over and trim him." The boys restrained him, and after the game mutual introductions followed between Duffy and McGuire. Duffy, still under the impression that McGuire was mocking him over his misfortune, sailed into the much astonished McGuire with all sails set. When we separated them and explained to Duffy that McGuire was afflicted just as he was, Duffy burst into tears and the two were inseparable on our next visit to Nashville. I have seen some great catchers in the game in Ewing, Bennet, Kling, Sullivan and others, and it is my sincere opinion that but for Duffy's unfortunate affliction he would rank with the best of them.

An Exciting Series.

HAVING disposed of my interests in the Charleston, S. C., club of the South Atlantic League, early in June, 1905, I assumed the management of the Scranton club of the New York State League. I found matters in bad shape at Scranton. The club was floundering around in last place with a shiftless lot of has-beens. This I remedied at once and we got out of the rut and were winning games with pleasing regularity. Our winning aroused the entire coal section to an enthusiasm it had never before enjoyed. The once-despised tailenders were now defeating all comers. A strong contender for the pennant that year was Scranton's sister city, Wilkesbarre. The rivalry between these cities was intense. Utica, A. J. & G. (Amsterdam, Johnstown and Gloversville) and Syracuse were right on the heels of Wilkesbarre. The season drifted on until the last week of the season, with Scranton and Wilkesbarre scheduled for the entire week. The excitement was tremendous. Crowds flocked to the games from the entire Anthracite Valley. Should Wilkes-Barre win four out of the seven games the pennant would be theirs, and the New York State clubs would be out of the running. In the first game on Monday my club went down to defeat by a close score, and the same on Tuesday and Wednesday. Loud cries of "laying down" could be heard on all sides. Dispatches from the New York State papers were copied by Wilkesbarre and Scranton papers. On Thursday my club had a little better luck, as we tied the Wilkesbarre team. Friday we played off the tie game of the day before and the worm turned, for we not only won that game, but the regular scheduled one also. This woke up the croakers. Saturday my team again defeated the now panicstricken Wilkesbarre outfit, and the result of the championship hinged upon the result of Sunday's game. By this time not only the cities of Wilkesbarre and Scranton were mad with excitement, but the entire league seemed to be in the same condition. Telegrams came pouring in to me from the other contenders, assuring me of their confidence in me and my club, and to keep up the good work. The fans of the two cities in the meantime were backing their favorite clubs to the limit. However, a new knocker had appeared upon the scene. "Will Scranton allow the pennant to go out of Pennsylvania?" shouted this one. "Never! my money goes on Wilkesbarre." The final game was played on Sunday at Minooka, a suburb of Scranton, to the largest crowd that ever witnessed a game in the Valley. The fans were fairly mad with enthusiasm. Wilkesbarre, suffering from the great

JAMES O'ROURKE
Member of the National Board

strain, went down before us in a rather easy manner. Scranton, the despised rival, who for years had been an easy victim on the ball field for the Wilkesbarreians, had dashed the pennant from the very grasp of its rivals. The feeling during the game, with partisans on both sides, was indescribable, and the play had to be stopped on numerous occasions to quell the outbursts. I really think that had I made my appearance in the city of Wilkesbarre that day after the game, I should have met with bodily harm.

However, Wilkesbarre fans are like all other fans, as forgiving as they are fickle, for in later years when I made my appearance with my club in that city, I was met with a hearty round of applause, evidently in recognition of the sterling honesty of those Wilkesbarre-Scranton games that had cost them a championship.

Humpty Badel.

WHEN I took charge of the Johnstown club of the Tri-State League in 1908 I had on my team a player by the name of "Humpty" Badel. The lad was a native of Pittsburg and was afflicted with quite a growth on his back, hence his sobriquet of "Humpty." Notwithstanding this misfortune, Badel was a ball player of ability. George Stallings induced him to leave the then outlaw Johnstown club and join his Buffalo club of the Eastern League in 1907. Stallings' club played several exhibition games during his spring trip at Cincinnati and Badel made such a grand showing in these games that Ned Hanlon, then manager of the Cincinnati club, offered Stallings $5,000.00 for his dwarf-looking right fielder. Stallings refused point blank, as he imagined he had a wonder. So he had, mechanically. How that lad Badel could hit! Short of stature, he had a crouching position at the bat that made him an exceedingly hard man to pitch to. He would meet the ball with a natural hard swing, had a wonderful eye and would offer only at good balls. On the bases he was a whirlwind, and in sliding he would invariably land on the "hump," making him an exceedingly hard man for the baseman to touch. He easily led the Tri-State League in base-running and run-getting, and it seemed a wonder to me why so grand a player was confined to a Class B. League. My experience with him at Johnstown soon convinced me that he belonged to that class and no higher. It was intellectually that Badel failed. It is always my custom to train my men in a system of signals whereby their team-work is carried through the season. In this inside work, Badel was absolutely helpless. He would do exactly the opposite of what he was told to do. He was willing enough, but was utterly unable to carry through anything pertaining to the inside department of the game. This often put him in bad with his fellow-players. He could not conceive the idea of the plays at all. Especially was he helpless in the code of signs and signals we had adopted. He was too valuable a player to release, so I took him in hand and instructed him in several verbal signals that we were to use in pulling off a play. To make the signs easy for him, I suggested that he name any words, numbers, etc., that I should tell him when a play was expected in which he might take part. To complicate the signs they were to be given by me in the German language. To play the hit-and-run-game, Badel suggested that I yell out and call him "Honus." He would then surely know what was expected of him. This I did, but soon everybody in the bleachers was calling him "Honus." He really got along well until one day, I put on the "Honus play" and Badel was so delighted in pulling it off that he yelled in to me on the coaching line in the German language, "Hab ich das nicht gesagt?" Then, notwithstanding my yells to look out for the ball that was being fast fielded in, he wandered off the base and was caught napping. There were not many more "Honus plays" after that, as poor Badel was seized with a nervous affliction and was compelled to quit the game. Thus closed the career of one of the greatest players of the present day, good enough for any club—minor or major league—mechanically.

A Stitch in Time.

ONE of minor league balldom's ablest promoters is my esteemed colleague, John J. Grim, of Cincinnati, Ohio. Grim's successes in the Northwest and in Virginia were notable. Grim is still the owner of a club in the Virginia League, but was not always a magnate. In 1904, Grim's Columbia, S. C., club of the South Atlantic League fell by the wayside for want of patronage. Grim accepted a position on the league's staff of umpires and finished the season as an arbitrator. In that position he was not without his troubles. My club was playing at Augusta, Ga., one day with Grim holding the indicator. He got along finely until my catcher, Sid. Smith, disputed a strike. Smith, who was later purchased by Connie Mack, was a hot-tempered young southerner, and went at Grim rather roughly with his language. He protested the decision vigorously, notwithstanding the fact that Grim had ordered him to keep quiet. Finally Grim lost patience. "That will cost you $5.00," said the now exasperated umpire. Here Smith completely lost his temper. "Fine me $5.00, will you?" he yelled starting toward Grim with the evident intention of assaulting him. Quick as a flash, when Jack saw him coming, he pulled his dust-broom out of his hip-pocket, and, vigorously dusting off the home plate, yelled to the fast on-coming Smith, "Back, back, go back, you busher! It's only a phoney fine."

Good or Bad Club?

IN 1907 I was at the head of the St. Paul club of the American Association, where I put in the most disastrous season of my career, finishing a hopeless last. The St. Paul's cognomen for years has been "The Saints." The home uniforms were a spotless and immaculate white; white caps, belts, trousers, shirts and white stockings.

St. Paul's greatest rival in baseball was its twin city, Minneapolis.

As is customary, the newspapers were comparing the relative strength of their respective teams. In the American Association we had on our umpire staff, one Perry Werden, a wit of great renown. When one of the Minneapolis scribes inquired of Perry as to the relative caliber of the Saints, Werden came back with this rather ambiguous reply, "Well, I'll tell you, they got dag-gone swell uniforms."

Home Runs to Order.

SOME years ago I acted in the capacity of coach for a Southern University. That year Connie Mack had several of his pitching squad down there, assisting me. With their aid I had the squad in pretty good shape and had drilled the boys into quite a team, notwithstanding the scarcity of players I had to select from. We were doing finely in coaching the boys but were sorely handicapped by an over-officious member of the faculty, who, no matter what we did, was ever offering a different suggestion. He capped the climax one day when he said to me: "Coach, I wish you would instruct the batsman, when all the bases are occupied, to hit the ball out yonder," pointing to the extreme center field fence—a half-mile off. I looked at him, thinking he was joshing, for here he was ordering up a home run as one would a bottle of beer or a cheese sandwich. No, the Professor was never more serious in his life. "Very well," I finally retorted; "as soon as the new consignment of bats that we ordered arrives, I will instruct the batsman to do so." This seemed to satisfy the officious one, for he worried us no more that day.

A Cruel Deception.

ONE of the characters very much missed in New York State League circles is Howard J. Earle, now doing scout duty for the Pittsburg club, of the National League. As a leader of minor league clubs Earle has been one of the most successful managers in the country. In fact, wherever Earle has appeared, he is beloved by all, and a more conscientious leader would be hard to find. Especially on the New York State League circuit he is revered by all fans, and many would like to see him occupy the presidential chair of this snug little organization. Throughout the circuit there is seldom a fanning bee where Earle's name is not mentioned. Many are the stories told on him. Earle played first base for his club in no slouchy manner, but it was at the bat that he excelled. While a very strong batsman he had a holy dislike for the spitball. In a game at Utica one day Earle faced Jack Flater, a noted spitball artist, who later was secured by Connie Mack's Athletic club. It was Earle's turn at bat, and the bases were all occupied. The first ball that Flater offered to Earle was met with a resounding whack and went into deep left field, but foul. The next ball Flater served was also fouled off by Earle. Then Flater commenced his strategy. The next three balls offered were wide of the plate, evidently to try and induce Earle to hit at a bad ball. It was now three balls and two strikes, and the real battle between batsman and pitcher was on. Flater stood in the box, apparently wetting the ball. When Earle observed Flater preparing to serve the spitter, it could be seen that he was becoming plainly nervous. Flater wound up but instead of delivering the expected spitball, he sent in a fast curve that shot directly over the plate. "Three strikes! you're out!" yelled the umpire. Earle was nonplussed and wellnigh speechless. All he said was: "Jack, you scamp, you lied to me."

In 1905 Earle won the pennant on the last day of the season after a hard and game fight. There were four clubs contending for the championship up to the very last day. While there was much disappointment among the three other contending clubs, there still was much rejoicing in league circles at Earle's hard-fought victory. Early that season Earle had the misfortune to have his shortstop injured and he was moving heaven and earth trying to replace him. Earle was naturally very much put out at his ill-luck, as was the president of the club, a Mr. Button, who did all in his power in assisting Earle to replace his injured player. One bright morning Pres. Button met Earle with a glad smile. "Howard," said the president, "shake hands. Our troubles are all over. I have here an application from a young man who doesn't drink, chew tobacco or smoke, just the man we want!" "Enough, enough, Mr. Button!" yelled Earle. "We don't want that fellow! Why, he isn't a ball player, he's a bookkeeper."

Chic Cargo, who a few years ago played shortstop on the Albany club of the New York league, had a funny one pulled off on himself by Howard Earle, who was then at the head of the Utica club.

There was a Utica man on first base when the batsman tried to bunt and advance the runner to second. The ball was fielded to the second baseman who seemingly held it, then dropped it. The umpire called him safe. Instantly there was an argument. They argued the decision pro and con. Finally somebody said he was out as the second baseman had held the ball momentarily. Quick as a flash Cargo (whose education was known by all the players to be limited) rushed up to the umpire and said: "Mr. Umpire, I claim the man is out! Didn't he hold the ball momentarily?" When Earle heard this he "got off" the umpire long enough to vent his wrath on Cargo. "Chick, who in the name of goodness ever told you of the word 'momentarily'! what do you know about that?" Then turning to the umpire Howard exclaimed: "Momentarily, ha, ha! Why, Mr. Umpire, this fellow Cargo can't count eleven. Momentarily, indeed." Everybody laughed, good-humor was restored, and the decision in favor of Utica stood.

The Bonehead.

IN a magazine article, Mr. Bozeman Bulger, of the New York *World*, gives me credit for originating the term "bonehead," which is now in general use for describing stupid plays on the diamond. Mr. Bulger's story is as follows:

Just who coined the word in baseball is a matter of wide discussion among baseball writers; but the man who is frequently credited with it is Eddie Ashenback, late manager of the Scranton, Pennsylvania, baseball team. Ashenback has been manager of many other ball clubs and is considered one of the great wits of the diamond. The first appearance of the word" bonehead" in baseball literature occurred some eleven years ago, and it so happened that the writer saw the incident that caused Ashenback to use it.

The baseball teams of Birmingham, Alabama, and Shreveport, Louisiana, were playing a game at Birmingham. Ashenback was manager of Shreveport. It was the last week of the season, and he was very short of players. In fact, he was so short that he hired a local semi-professional player named McGowan to take the position of right field for the one game.

"Can you play outfield?" Ashenback asked of the ambitious youngster.

"Sure," he replied. "I can play anywhere, and I can show a lot of these leaguers up, too."

"Well, get on that glove and go out to right field," was Ashenback's order.

During the practice McGowan did very well, and Ashenback seemed somewhat relieved. The youngster made several nice catches.

The game finally started, and the Birmingham club had two runners on bases. The next man up drove a high fly into right field. McGowan started for the ball; but somehow he lost his nerve and was unable to judge its direction correctly. He made three or four circles, and finally gave up entirely just as the ball came down, struck him on the head, and bounded to a far corner of the lot for three bases. Both runners scored, and Ashenback was wild.

"Here you boneheaded mutt, come here!" he yelled at the top of his voice to McGowan. Then, picking up a catcher's mask, the irate manager ran out from the bench toward the middle of the diamond to meet the disgraced right fielder. "Here, you bonehead," he yelled, "take this mask and put it on, or they'll knock your brains out with the first fly they put over!"

The spectators heard the entire dialogue, or rather monologue, and roared with laughter. The story happened to fall to my lot and it was sent all over the country. That was the first time I heard the use of the word "bonehead."

The incident described is perfectly accurate, but I first made use of the term some years previous to the game mentioned by Mr. Bulger. I'll tell you just how I came by the word. In 1899 I played center field for the Springfield, Ohio, club. On the team were Josh Reilly, third baseman, now retired and deputy coroner of San Francisco, and a catcher to whom we gave the nickname of Zeekoe, and who was continually doing just the opposite of what he was instructed to do. He had a serious weakness, in that it was utterly impossible for him to catch a high foul fly. He would dance under the ball until he got dizzy. Reilly often advised that we build a wooden shed over him, so that his head would not be shattered by one of those high fouls. One day the expected happened. The ball went high up into the air, with Zeekoe, as usual, doing his sky-dance, under it. It finally landed, not in his mitt, but right on top of his head, bouncing fully thirty feet off his bean into the bleachers. The blow would have felled an ox. Down went poor Zeekoe, but only for an instant —to pick up his mask, which had been knocked off in the encounter. That evening, in the dining-room, Reilly and I passed Zeekoe, who was enjoying his evening meal with the utmost complacency. In passing him, I playfully pressed both of my hands on his head to feel for the bump which a blow of that kind should have raised. The lump was conspicuous by its absence. "Are you hurt?" I inquired of him. "Not a bit," he said with pride. Turning to Reilly, I remarked, "No wonder, Josh, that he isn't hurt. His head is of solid bone." I believe this was the very first use of the term. Ever since that night I have applied the expression "bonehead" to any player guilty of unusual stupidity, and it has gained wide circulation.

Some Boneheaded Plays.

MAN on first base, nobody out, batsman hits for a home run, yet nobody scores. Impossible? No! just a "bone play" by the base-runner, and a witty quick-thinking second baseman. It happened in the old Inter-State League. Mansfield was playing our club at New Castle, Pa. Pop Lytle, our manager, was on first base with nobody out. Joe Rickert was at bat and the hit-and-run play was put on. On the ball pitched, Lytle, with head down and all speed set, started to second base. Rickert hit the ball an awful swipe to the right field fence. When Lytle arrived near second base with head down, he beheld second baseman Werrick, of the Mansfield club, gazing up into the air as if he were waiting for the ball to descend. Upon seeing this, Lytle, imagining Rickert had really hit the ball in the air, turned and tried to get back to first base to avoid a double play. In turning he collided with the fast flying Rickert and down they both went. By the time they had recovered from the collision and dragged themselves back to first and second base, Rickert's home run drive had been fielded in. This left the two men on the bases. The next batsman hit into a double play and the last man was an easy out. Werrick's heady play had turned what promised to be a disastrous inning for his club into a possible victory. Lytle, amid the jibes of his teammates and the audience, sneaked back to the bench, and promised to let the players shoot him if ever he fell again at the hands of the tricky Werrick. Poor

Lytle! Werrick was too much for him, for in the very next series he and Rickert again tried to pull off the hit and run play on Werrick. Lytle was on first base when Rickert gave him the signal for the play. As the pitcher delivered the ball, Lytle, again, with head down, started for second base. Arriving there, he saw the tricky Werrick evidently in the act of fielding an imaginary ground ball. Into second base slid Lytle, arising smilingly and brushing the dust off his uniform. He started to josh Werrick. Rickert had popped up a little fly to the third baseman, who while Lytle slid into second and was joshing Werrick, threw the ball to first base, easily doubling him up on the play.

This was the finish of Lytle as playing manager of the club, as the directors of the team absolutely refused to furnish him with a geography to aid him in running the bases.

The players in the Tri-State League always delighted in pulling off these plays on Billy Clay and an outfielder named Perry. Clay was the official conversationalist of the League. Reaching first base in a game, the first baseman, aware of Bill's weakness for getting his mind off the game, would start on Clay. "Bill, how's the family, and your old man? You were sure hitting that ball down at Trenton, eh, boy?" When you mentioned hits to Clay, you had his weakness. He would become interested to such an extent that he forgot all about his being on the base. All of a sudden the catcher, from a quick signal from the first baseman, would throw the ball down to first base and catch poor Clay napping ten feet off the base, still gossiping about his hits and the folks at home. Whenever Perry reached first base with one or no one out, I always instructed my baseman, after an out, to take his glove off, throw it on the ground and start toward the players' bench. "Three out, whose time is it at bat?" the player would yell. Perry, thinking the side was retired, would walk out to his position in the field only to be nabbed by one of my men.

Retribution.

BILL SMINK, well known in Eastern League circles, and pitcher Con Lucid were the participants in a most ridiculous affair at Hartford, Conn., in a game in 1896. Smink was an inveterate umpire-baiter, and on this day seemed worse than ever. He fairly tore the clothes off the arbitrator. All this time Lucid was on the bench snorting his disgust at Smink's actions and imploring the umpire to remove him from the game. The umpire was not blessed with an over-abundance of backbone and allowed Smink to abuse him almost at will. Finally Lucid could stand for Smink's actions no longer. Reaching down into his manager's valise he seized a couple of balls, and hurled one with full force at the abusing Smink. The ball hit him in the small of the back with a resounding whack. Smink turned around to see who had hit him, when Lucid let go with terrific force and caught Smink full in the mouth. Down went Smink in a heap, scattering his store-teeth in all directions. It was an awful blow. The boys picked Smink up, and sent him out to a physician to be patched up, who advised that he be shipped on home, as it would be some time before he would be able to get back into the game. Smink was put on a train and duly arrived at home. Upon his arrival he had occasion to visit the ball grounds, where he was met by the groundkeeper, who nearly had a fit when he beheld Smink's battered face. "Good hi'vins, Bill," exclaimed the Celt; "what happened to yez?" "Bu! Bu! Got hit in the mouth with a ball," spluttered Smink, out of his badly battered and swollen mouth. "Well, thin, Bill!" retorted the badly shocked groundkeeper, "for the love of hivin, Bill, haven't they got the ball out yit?"

Let 'em Alone.

TIM FLOOD succeeded me as manager of the St. Paul club in 1908. Tim had about the same luck with the Saints that I did, and finished at the bottom of the ladder. Tim could not get his club started, it seems. After losing eleven consecutive games at the opening of the season, the Saints arrived in Kansas City to do battle for a series of games. They entered the grounds on the first day of the series to do or die. They went after the Kansas City pitcher full of ginger and batted him all over the lot. With the score 9 to 1 in favor of St. Paul it really looked as if the Saints had at last broken their long string of defeats. Phil Geier, who made his debut in the major league with Lajoie, was then a member of the St. Paul club, while Jake Beckley played first base for the Kansas City club. "Well, well, Phil," ejaculated Beckley, "it really looks as if you fellows had broken the ice and will win a game today." "Hold on, Jake," returned Geier. "Not so fast! Just let us alone, let us alone, I tell you! Don't bother us! We'll beat ourselves, if you only let us alone!" Sure enough, Geier was right. With a combination of hits and errors by the Saints the Kansas City club won out and the poor luckless Saints went down to another defeat.

Penurious Players.

IT was an old-time fanning bee at the National Association meeting in Chicago not long ago. The subject of course was the players and their various idiosyncrasies and the penurious habits possessed by some of them. "I knew a guy once in the Western League," said umpire Steve Cusack, "who knew every lunch station in the entire league. At meal time he would collect his dollar from the manager and at the first stop, instead of going into the dining room, would hike out and get a couple of sandwiches." "That is nothing," said Charley Schaefer, the St. Joe manager, "I had an infielder who had a peculiar habit of falling off in his work on the home grounds. You have heard of players going to beat the band when on their own dunghill but falling off in their work on the road. Not so with this fellow. I did

TWO PHILADELPHIA PILGRIMS
Cartoonist Hoban and Sporting Editor Graham of the North American.

not know what to think of his queer ailment and decided to investigate. 'There is no use of your investigating anything. I will tell you what is the matter,' said one of my pitchers. 'Why, this fellow is so stingy that he does not supply himself with the proper necessities of life. Come to dinner with us tomorrow and I will convince you.' Sure enough the next day we went down to the restaurant where the mysterious infielder dined and there he was with coffee and rolls in front of him. On the road it was quite different. In all the hotels he had the waiters crippled carrying in food. The first few days on the road this fellow went like a house on fire but toward the close of the trip he would fall off in his work. He loaded up so on foodstuffs that he could hardly navigate, evidently laying in a supply for the next trip at home."

"That is nothing at all," spoke up Jack Tighe, the Spokane manager. "There was a fellow in the National League some years ago who had them all skinned. Why, this lad was so tight that nothing short of a regiment of blackhanders could make him loosen up. He would borrow your razor to shave. He was never known to buy a newspaper or even a postage stamp. He wouldn't buy you a cigar at the point of a revolver. All the waiters on the circuit were next to him and gave him a wide berth upon his entry to the dining room." When Tighe finished, Tom Connery, the clever manager of the Hartford, Conn., team, spoke up. "I heard all your stories of them 'spendthrifts' and I guess I will have to disperse this fanning bee with the one I am going to tell you.

"I had a fellow down in Connecticut that I dug up somewhere in the Maine woods. It did not take his teammates long to become aware of the fact that the Maine woodsman was as stingy as they make them. Notwithstanding his penurious habits, the woodsman was a very religious chap and every Sunday found him at service at the church. Now this woodsman was a constable in his Maine town, and, at the services, when the contribution box was handed around, instead of contributing his mite, he nearly knocked the breath out of a pair of his teammates by pulling back his coat and showing his badge."

Connery put the fanning bee to rout with this one and they fought shy of him during the rest of the meeting.

A Plea for Sunday Ball.

DID you ever see the croaker who is continually bewailing the terrible misfortune of being compelled to have his home city numbered among the ones that play Sunday ball? He may may be a merchant, a saloon-keeper, or more likely some misguided preacher who has never been six feet away from his sanctum in his life, thus missing the health-giving exercise indulged in by playing our great national game. Does the merchant ever think that the very fact of his home team playing games is a distinct benefit to him, also to the inn-keeper? In many towns and cities, especially in the middle west,

Sunday excursions are run to see a game of ball on the Sabbath. Tens of thousands of these excursionists are carried in by the railroads to those cities that tolerate a game on the first day of the week. To the inn-keeper and merchant I will say, "Where are these Sunday excursionists accommodated in the matter of nourishment, etc.?" Why, at his inn, of course. The inn-keeper is happy, for he has all he can do to accommodate his visitors. Still he is crying about Sunday baseball. Were it not for this innocent amusement, these excursionists would not only be conspicuous by their absence, but his own people would probably get into the habit of going elsewhere, where the game is played on Sunday, thus not only depriving him of his former revenue, but carrying their money elsewhere. In the coal regions of Pennsylvania, notably in Wilkesbarre, Scranton, Pottsville and Shamokin, Sunday baseball is tolerated with pleasure by the populace, and is heartily welcomed by members of the church. Of course there was some agitation anent the game. Right Reverend Archbishop Hoban came out openly advocating Sunday baseball, stating that his parishioners were fully entitled to the bright sunshine and the exercise that they were able to indulge in but one day of the week and that the Sabbath. The Sunday games at Scranton are played at Minooka, a suburb of the city, and it is no secret that the chief of police of the little burg has resigned since the playing of games on Sunday. To the hard-working miner who enters his mine sometimes at daybreak and leaves long after dark, a game of baseball on Sunday is a boon not long to be forgotten, and to deprive him of his one pastime is more than a cruelty. To the whining, crying preacher—with all due respect—I will say, I have yet to see in the Bible where the Great Umpire expects one to be on his knees all day Sunday.

Buying A Youngster.

ONE of the greatest cases of gold-bricking in the history of baseball transactions was pulled off by Walter Wilmot, the old Chicago outfielder and now a leader in the automobile business, when he was managing the Butte club, of the Northwestern League in 1905. Wilmot had a first baseman by the name of Charley Shaffer, known as Nickelnose, on account of the peculiar and beautiful curve of his proboscis. Shaffer hit 346 and led the league in fielding in 1904, helping materially in winning the pennant for his club. His high averages, both in batting and fielding, attracted the attention of President John I. Taylor of the Boston Americans, who entered into negotiations for this star youngster and bought him at a fancy price. Mr. Taylor was full of praise for the young star that he had picked up and assured all his friends that he had found a wonder who would surely make good. He thought so well of Nickel-nose that he sent him $500 advance money and transportation to Washington, D. C., where he joined the Boston team in March, 1905, while the club was on its way to Macon to train. There was a lot of interest in the promising young recruit and the players were lined up in the hotel lobby to take a look at him when he came in. One look was enough for Lachance, Gibson, Stahl, Collins, Cy Young and Criger, all of whom had played against Shaffer about twelve years before. They could scarcely believe their eyes when they saw Nickel-nose proudly waltzing in to report in the guise of a young comer. But the old players were good sports and never let on. Shaffer went to playing with the yannigans as shortstop and captain and none but the veterans knew that he was not a kid just getting his first try-out, though he had been playing ball for more than a dozen years. One of the Boston scribes who was making the southern trip with the club took Shaffer very seriously and attempted to improve his style at the bat, hoping by his advice to make a hitter out of him.

One day Shaffer was up in a practice game, with the bases full in the last half of the ninth and four runs needed to win the game. Jess Tannehill was pitching for the regulars and Burkett was playing left field. Jess tipped Nickel-nose off that he was going to send in a straight, fast ball directly over the plate. Shaffer, knowing just what was coming, set himself, hit the ball a mile over Burkett's head for a homer and won the game for the yannigans. As soon as he had scored, he walked over to the press box and said to the reporter who had been criticising his manner at the bat, "You see, old boy, that it is not style but execution that counts while at the bat."

The secret was too good to keep and President Taylor finally found out that he had been harboring an alleged youngster who had been in the minor leagues for many years. Mr. Taylor, who is a thorough sportsman, took it in good part. Shaffer had made a hit with his crazy coaching, and Mr. Taylor was willing to carry him through the season just to see him out on the lines, but finally decided to sell him to Savannah, where he managed the team and finished second in the race.

Shaffer has made good in baseball and is now manager of the St. Joe club, of the Western League, but he never tires of telling about his try-out as a youngster with the Boston Americans.

A Sturdy Veteran.

THE oldest active ball player in the country today is that grand character, James H. O'Rourke, of Bridgeport, Conn., who has just completed his forty-fourth year of service on the diamond. Mr. O'Rourke began playing with an amateur team as a boy in 1867, and he has never had an off-year since that time. In his long career he has played in every position on the field, from catcher all the way around to right-fielder, but it was as a catcher with the Boston Reds and the New York Giants that he attained his greatest fame.

Jim O'Rourke is a native of Bridgeport, where he still lives. He began playing ball there in 1867 with an amateur team called the Unions. For the next four years he was with another amateur club called the Oceolas, of Stratford, Conn., three miles from Bridgeport. In 1872 he was with Middletown, Tim Murnane and John Clapp being members of the club at the same time. For the next six years he was with the old Boston Red Stockings, under the management of Harry Wright, and helped the team win the championship in five of those six seasons. In 1874 he accompanied the Bostons to England. The Athletics of Philadelphia also made the trip and the two clubs played both baseball and cricket for the edification of the Britishers. In a throwing competition at the Oval, in London, in which he had for opponents members of the Boston and Philadelphia teams and also some Englishmen, Mr. O'Rourke was awarded a handsome prize for winning the contest, in which both a baseball and a cricket ball had to be thrown.

In 1879 Mr. O'Rourke was a member of the Providence team, which was managed by George Wright. The next year he went back to Boston, but in 1881 he went to the Buffalo club as manager, captain and player. His last year at Buffalo gave him the honor of leading the batsmen of the National League. From 1885 to 1892 inclusive, he was with the New York Giants, with the exception of one season, that of 1890, when he cast in his lot with the players in the Brotherhood movement. In 1893 he was with the Washington club as manager, captain and player, and this concluded his work in the National League, with which he had been closely identified for a period of twenty-one years.

Having retired on his laurels from the National League, Mr. O'Rourke played in 1894 with the St. Joseph club of Bridgeport, and the following year he organized the Naugatuck Valley League.

In 1895 he organized the Connecticut League, which is in existence today and is one of the strongest and best Class B leagues in the land. Until a year or two ago, Mr. O'Rourke played regularly with his club at Bridgeport, of which he is the owner, and the fans enjoyed the unusual sight of seeing him catch game after game while his son played third base on the same team. For a couple of years he has not been so active as a player, but always works in a few games and is still active on his feet and a first-class hitter.

Mr. O'Rourke has not lost any opportunities to advance in his profession. From an amateur ballplayer on the lots, he has become a club-owner, a promoter, and a magnate. He is one of the ablest and most honored members of the National Board, the executive committee of the huge National Association, where his advice and judgment are considered of the highest value.

He graduated from the law department of Yale University in 1887 and for more than twenty years has conducted a flourishing legal practice in his home town. He is a unique character in the national game and an honor to the noble sport.

Ramsey's Mustache.

HANK RAMSEY, one of the chief organizers of the New York State League, used to be very fond of a little hirsute adornment on his upper lip. During a game of ball when his club was in a fair way to win, Hank would fondly caress his mustache.

HUMOR AMONG THE MINORS

When his club was behind, Hank would attack it until it was a wonder he did not pull it out by the roots. Ramsey's antics on the bench with his mustache were by no means lost upon the bleacherites. "Say, Hank," they would yell. "What is that below your nose? A wire brush?" "No, you mutt. It's his eyebrow that slipped below his nose." Hank always took this chaff in good spirit until one day at Scranton. His club was playing Binghamton that day. Before the game the batteries as usual were warming up as Hank strolled toward his place on the bench, fondly caressing and twirling his mustache, when, bang! a stray ball thrown by Bob Drury, the manager of the Binghamton club, hit him fully in the mouth. It was an awful blow, and Hank went down like an ox. He was out in a day or so, but his face was swelled out of all proportions. The merciless bleachers were still after him, however, and they yelled, "Go to some nickel barber-shop, Hank, and have it amputated. It looks like a handle bar on a bicycle." Very reluctantly he decided to part with his pet mustache. His Scranton club was defeated by a very small margin for the pennant that season, by a "hairsbreadth," his players claim. Since then Ramsey has discarded his pet. "It was a Jonah, at that," he exclaims, for he won the first pennant for Altoona later in a runaway race, and he attributes the grand showing of his club to the amputation of his treasure.

Lost.

ON a scouting expedition through the Tri-State League some time ago, President Watkins of Indianapolis, arrived at Trenton, N. J., and was very much struck by the able performance in the box of a left-handed pitcher by the name of "Lefty" Craig. He lost no time in entering into negotiations with the Trenton people for the release of the crack pitcher. Terms were agreed upon and as the Tri-State League closed its season rather early, Mr. Watkins stipulated that Craig be sent on to Indianapolis immediately upon the close of the Tri-State League. This would give him an opportunity to try out his newly-purchased pitcher and get a good line on his ability for the following season. As soon as Craig's fellow-players learned of his sale he became the butt of their joshing and jokes. Craig was anything but well up in geography and the boys soon had him believing he would have to cross an ocean and a couple of continents to reach Indianapolis. Just before the close of the Tri-State season, Manager Heckert made preparations to send Craig on to Indianapolis as per his agreement with President Watkins. But, no, it was no Indianapolis for Craig. Manager Heckert begged and implored him to be on his way to join the Indianapolis club. But to no avail. Finally Heckert prevailed upon Craig to explain his refusal to join Mr. Watkins' club. Craig told Heckert all his teammates had said about far-off Indianapolis. The joshing of his teammates was explained to Craig, who was really becoming anxious to enter upon his new duties. However, Manager Heckert took no chances with the bright left-hander, but secured transportation for himself and Craig and the pair arrived in the Hoosier City in due time, where Craig made quite a hit. But for Heckert's companionship, he would never have dared set out on the journey.

On my Altoona club in 1909 I had a husky pitcher named Dowdell whom I picked up in the wilds of Kentucky. We were on our way north from Virginia and had just arrived in Philadelphia from Baltimore. I sent the club on ahead, being detained by some business in Baltimore. I gave Dowdell my baggage to attend to on the trip north and he took such elegant care of the valise that he did not let it out of his view. In Philadelphia one of the jokesmiths of the club told him he had just received a telegram ordering him (Dowdell) not to move off the spot until the arrival of his manager. The poor Kentuckian waited and waited, but of course no Manager Ashenback showed up. When two or three days passed on and no Dowdell made his appearance, I became alarmed and set some Philadelphia police friends to look him up. The hunt was not a long one, for at Broad St. Station in Philadelphia, where the jokesmith had told him to await his arrival, was the faithful Kentuckian, still awaiting the arrival of his manager.

Sullivan's Clever Ways.

CAN you remember the bitterest hour you ever spent in your life? I can. It was way back in 1892. That spring Ted Sullivan was recruiting his Chattanooga club in Cincinnati. Ted arrived in the Queen City and stopped at the Grand Hotel, and as soon as his arrival became known, every ballplayer in the city was beseeching him for a position. Amongst them was myself. Among that crowd in waiting I guess I was the most timid. I finally approached Mr. Sullivan and asked him for a position. Ted picked me up and in an evidently joking manner told me that he would sign me as soon as he received a supply of contracts. As the desk in Sullivan's room was fairly loaded down with contracts it dawned on me that I was being made the butt of a practical joke. I left Sullivan determined to make him give me a chance. In some manner the players who were in waiting became aware of Sullivan's little joke, and my appearance amongst them was met with shouts of laughter and ridicule. "Here come the contracts," shouted one wag, as a big transfer wagon drove by us. With a heavy heart I determined then and there that I would make a success in my chosen profession. Ted left for Chattanooga in due time with his players, and I followed on a fast freight train, determined to get a place on his team. I arrived in Chattanooga after a strenuous journey, and was met with more laughter and ridicule by the players from my home town. "How did you get here, Ash? Did you swim over the mountains?" and other jibes were hurled my way. When Sullivan beheld me he evidently realized he had played his joke too far. With a little fatherly advice, he told me that while his team was now complete, he would take care of me as soon as the opportunity presented itself. Ted, as usual, was as good as his word. The following winter he hunted me up and signed me for his Atlanta club of the Southern League. The year following I was also with Sullivan, so I am quite sure Ted made ample retribution for his little joke on an ambitious youngster. What became of my abusers? Oh! they are engaged in various positions. One is driving a dump-wagon and the others are not much better off. It was just such little acts as this of rewarding persistence with a position that made Ted Sullivan. His success as a promoter stands second to none in baseballdom. The leagues he organized are too numerous to mention, and hundreds of players owe their livelihood to him.

In the games Ted would always appear in uniform and coach his men from the lines. His "Texas Steer" club had such a lead for the pennant at Dallas in 1895, that he would very frequently play in the game himself. One day at San Antonio Ted announced that he would pitch. We all looked upon this as a joke, but sure enough into the box went Ted. The San Antonio team fairly ran into themselves getting up to the plate for a shot at Ted's curves, but inning after inning went by with Ted still in the box. Ted and the umpire, who was working behind the pitcher, were fairly bursting with hilarity. "Here comes Bullet-proof Ned," Ted would shout, as a San Antonio batsman would appear at the plate. The batsman would grit his teeth and go out on an easy fly ball. The San Antonio batsmen, in fact, all of us, commenced to wonder how an old chap like Ted could last an entire game. However, Ted's and the umpire's hilarity soon became plain to us, for foxy Ted had sneaked up fully ten feet toward the batsman in the pitcher's box. Pitching from only fifty feet, he was able to keep the sluggers from hitting the ball and he was having a lot of fun out of it.

In another game at San Antonio Ted had quite an afternoon with Crazy Schmidt, who was pitching for the Bronchos. Ted was constantly getting after the big German pitcher. The Bronchos were composed mostly of youngsters and the game was replete with errors. In one inning one of our men hit to the shortstop who threw wild. The next batsman hit an easy fly that was dropped and another fly ball was also dropped, filling the bases. All this time Ted was shouting at Schmidt. The next batsman hit a fly to the infield. All the infielders rushed after it. "Get avay," shouted Schmidt at the top of his voice. "Get avay." The infielders got out of Schmidt's way, down came the ball, but instead of catching it, he stooped down in a crouching position and let the ball hit him in the back. When the San Antonio manager remonstrated with him, Schmidt said, "Vat is de difference iff I get hit mit de ball? Didn't effery man on de infielt get a rap on de coco? Vat is de difference iff I get one on de 'bonnet'?" Schmidt later went to Baltimore with McGraw. In one game his manager was ejected. Schmidt, who was coaching on third base, threw all kinds of handsprings and somersaults on the coaching lines, until he too finally was ejected from the game. McGraw's team, notwithstanding his ejection, won the game. Schmidt's hilarity at the victory knew no bounds. He rushed up to the umpire gleefully shouting, "By Gott, Mr. Umpire, you are to be congratulated. You strengthened the whole Baltimore team by putting McGraw and me out of de game."

Homer.

AN expression frequently used among ball players, especially the visiting clubs, and addressed to the umpire, is the term "Homer," signifying that that official usually favors the home club in his decisions. Of course this is all bosh, but the word is used in general by all the players throughout the country. Podge Alloway, a husky Kentuckian, who formerly was a minor league pitcher of some note, a few years ago was handling the indicator in a little league in Kansas. After an unusually strenuous game one day, Alloway wandered back to his hotel, weary and sick in body and mind. He seated himself in a chair in front of the hotel at the conclusion of his evening meal, to rest and meditate over his hard day's work, when the visiting players on their way to the depot passed him on the opposite side of the street. As soon as they espied Alloway, their wrath over his alleged poor work arose again. "Homer, homer, oh, you rotten homer," they yelled. At this juncture the tired and much-abused Kentuckian jumped out of his chair and shouted at the retreating visitors, "Look eeh, you-all scamps, my name h'aint Homer. It's Alloway."

A Pair of Night Riders.

AT Memphis some years ago Ted Sullivan had a night ride that he did not forget for quite a while. On his team he had that pair of Irish rogues, Jack McCarthy, later with Cincinnati and Chicago, and Jack Tighe, now a successful manager out west. Whether by design or by mistake, these two worthies entered Ted's room one bright moonlight night. Here was Ted, reposing with his gray bald head shining in the moonlight, when bang! down came McCarthy's hand with a resounding smack right on Ted's dome. Ted jumped up out of bed furious, and sailed into these two giants. When he was finally quieted he said, "I hope yez two spalpeens will forgive me for waking up. I wish to at least apologize to so fine a pair of gentlemen as the pair of you."

The "Jerries."

HERE, you baseball enthusiasts, did you ever hear of the "Jerries"? Of course not. The term is used in baseball parlance by the players for those who are addicted to strong drink. "Do you remember Erve Beck, Ash?" inquired Ed McKernan the hustling manager of the Paris, Ky., club of the Blue Grass League. "Yes, sure I do," I replied. "Well, I'll tell you a funny one about him—and it's the gospel truth. When the Cincinnati club released him, he joined the Augusta, Ga., team. It was evident when he reported that there

ASHENBACK'S RECORD-BREAKING TEAM

was something amiss with him. In the games at Augusta I was playing second base while Beck was holding down first base. 'Shoo, shoo!' Beck would say, chasing an imaginary flock of geese away from the base. 'Look at the birds in the water.' A lot of such imaginary stuff he would pull off. It was evident that Beck was afflicted with some ailment or other and a physician was consulted. Sure enough, Beck had the 'Jerries,' and complete rest was prescribed for him. One night at the hotel, Beck in his delirium, went head-first out of a third-story window, and came crashing out on the sidewalk. That finished his baseball career. During his convalescence his fellow-players would visit him and Beck would smilingly avow his determination to abstain from strong drink in the future, and would then go on and describe his hallucinations during the fits of the 'Jerries,' much to the laughter of his fellow-players. 'But,' I asked him, 'why in the name of Joseph did you jump out of the third story window?' 'Well, I'll tell you, Mc,' said Beck, 'I imagined that somebody shot a message into that room containing the word "Get" and I got.'"

A Somnambulistic Player.

ED SHORTELL, who so cleverly captained the Altoona club of the Tri-State League into the championship recently, had quite an experience some years ago while a member of the Syracuse club of the New York State League. The team that year contained a number of rather old players who would loaf and avoid sliding into the bases when occasion required. Of course there were quite a few instances when they would have made the desired base had they slid, and many a run was lost through their failure to "hit the dirt." Manager Griffin of the Syracuse club was loud in his denunciations of his players for failing to slide. "You fellows will have to slide, or it will cost you some money," he would say. He kept preaching, "Slide, slide, slide," until even the oldest members of the club actually became frisky and slid into the bases. One night at Syracuse, Shortell had retired rather early, when an awful crash came from his room. Ed was a confirmed somnambulist and frequently would make night excursions in his sleep. This night Ed evidently had had his stroll, for, returning to his room, he went head foremost into a large mirror. The boys fished him out of the wreck, much tattered and torn, slightly slashed and cut, but not hurt seriously. "What in the name of blazes did you do?" asked some of the boys. "Are you going dippy?" "Dippy your neck," retorted the half-asleep Shortell. "That guy Griffin has been preaching sliding so long that I took a header through the mirror in my sleep." The Syracuse club always "hit the dirt" after that incident.

Quite a Managerial Record.

THERE is a red-headed scamp at Wilkesbarre who once licked me for the pennant the very last week of the season in the New York State League. However, I contented myself with second place in the race, and am now going to tell you of an aggressive manager who has been continually knocking at the door of the major leagues for admission. If the records are a criterion, the door should have been opened for him long ago.

After playing professional ball since the year 1892, William J. Clymer entered the managerial ranks at Wilkesbarre in 1900. His first effort resulted in bringing his club home in second place. In 1901 Bill went to Buffalo, and in 1902-1903 to Louisville, Ky., in the American Association, and finished second both years. Clymer maintained the good showing that he made with the Louisville club when he transferred his operations to Columbus, Ohio, by finishing second there in 1904. It was in 1905th at Clymer's wonderful ability shone, for not only that season did he win the pennant, but the two following years of 1906-1907 also. This feat of winning three straight pennants has seldom been equaled in any league, and Clymer has the distinction of being the only manager who ever won three consecutive pennants in a Class A League. In 1908 Bill was again at Columbus and he finished a good third, and landed the same position in 1909. In 1910 Clymer severed his long connection with the Columbus club and purchased the Wilkesbarre club, which is a veritable gold mine.

Here Bill again won the pennant, making the remarkable record of finishing second four times, third twice, and winning four championships in ten years of service.

Clymer is a hustler in all that the word implies. He is on the field leading his men at all times. As a coacher he has no equal and his buzz-saw voice is heard all over the grounds. His grand record shows conclusively that he is a manager of marked ability, one who has always brought his club in 1-2-3, and were big league managerial positions secured on the strength of one's record, Clymer should have had a front seat on the major league band wagon long ago. The date is not far distant when he will be selected to handle one of the major league clubs, for any manager who can lead an American Association club on to the championship for three consecutive years is worthy of some major league consideration.

Did Not Need Third Baseman.

"WE were playing at Kansas City one day in 1903 when I was leading the Louisville club," said Bill Clymer, the popular owner of the Wilkesbarre Club, "and we put out a man with eight men, instead of having the full nine in action. Wish Eagan was pitching for me and Frank Foreman, the old National League pitcher, was umpiring. Sutor Sullivan was my third baseman, and an argument over balls and strikes arose between Eagan and Foreman. The latter was working behind the pitcher and the two were having it out for fair. I was playing left field that day, and looking in toward the diamond saw third base unoccupied and my third baseman Sullivan loitering around the pitcher's box. The batsman in the meantime flew out to the outfield, and when I yelled in from the field, 'What are you doing there, Sully? Get back to your position,' he called back, 'Wait a minute, Bill, I want to see which one of these two countrymen wins the argument.'"

Clymer is the author of the following baseball conundrum, the play having actually taken place in a game in the American Association: There are three men on the bases with one man out. Batter hits the ball to fair territory. There is no hit, no error, two assists, one put out, yet three runs score. ANSWER: Batter hits the ball to the right field fence, but fails to touch first base. Right-fielder relays the ball to second base and he relays to first base. The batter does not get a hit, but all three runs score.

A Large Crowd.

THE Williamsport Club of the Tri-State League was always noted for the crack teams it put in the field. In 1908 especially they had a great team with Harry Wolverton, manager and third base; Pete Lister, first base; Shean, now of Boston, second base; Eddie Foster, now with the

New York Americans, shortstop; Tom O'Hara, Joe Hennessey and Birdie Cree, now with the New York Americans, in the outfield; Jack Townsend; Warhop, now with the New York Americans; Ollie Briton and Jack Flater, later with the Athletics, pitchers.

The team was dubbed the "Millionaires," as about half a dozen rich men financed the club. The town was notorious for its light attendance. About the only vehicles at the game were a row of automobiles containing the "millionaires." The crowd seldom numbered over 200. Williamsport and Harrisburg, intense rivals on the ball field, that year fought for the pennant toward the latter part of the season. Harrisburg was scheduled at Williamsport for the final series of the season, and upon the result of these games the pennant hinged. The entire city of Williamsport was aroused over the outcome of these games, and it really looked as if the town would at last have a record-breaking crowd. There was also much interest displayed as to the attendance by the other clubs in the League. The games were played, Williamsport winning. One of my players, much interested as to the attendance, asked Manager Wolverton of the Williamsport club, "How did you fellows draw in those deciding games, Harry? What was the crowd?" Before Wolverton could reply the irrepressible Kid Foster answered for him: "The crowd? Oh! Mrs. Warhop, that's all."

A Queer Weakness.

WHAT do you think of a pitcher who has the speed of a Waddell and the cunning of a Plank, in fact, has as much ability, if not more, than some of the star left-handers of the present day, and yet must be content with a minor league berth? Yet such a man is Coveleskie, who "spilled the beans" for McGraw the very last week of the pennant race, at the Polo grounds in 1908, when the Giants went down before his prowess in all three games he pitched. In 1907 I had the Johnstown, Pa., club of the Tri-State League and one day we were playing Lancaster. Coveleskie was pitching for Lancaster and I never saw such speed and curves. I was on the first base line coaching. They had us 4 to 0 and the way Cove was going, chances for a run looked bad indeed. The game was getting late, and I started after Cove. "Vera-gava nay-doh-bray, ver-seek-nay-doh-bray," I let go at him in the Polish language. Cove looked at me from the box. "Shut up, you big-headed Dutchman!" he said, leaving the pitcher's box and walking over to me, threatening dire harm. It was then I started after him for fair, as he showed me by his action in threatening me that he was exceedingly thin-skinned. "Nay-doh-bray, Vera-gava" (No good, Big-headed) and a lot of other gibberish that I did not understand myself, I hurled at Cove. Lancaster's lead of four runs did not look so big with Cove pitching after that. He turned his attention to me instead of to the game. Three or four men in succession went to first base on balls, and a hit drove in two runs. Pandemonium reigned in the bleachers which contained quite a number of Polish miners. They took up my cries and you would imagine the game was being played somewhere in Poland. All this time Coveleskie was prancing around in the box hardly knowing his whereabouts. "Here, make that fat-headed Dutchman quit hollering at me," he appealed to Tom Connors, formerly of the American League, who was umpiring; "he's calling me names in Polish." "Make 'im quit yerself," replied Connors. "Begorra! I'm Irish, I'm no Dago, and I can't understand yer Blackhand language. The Dutchman may be singing for all I know. Go in there and take yer medicine." Poor Cove was now completely gone. We soon tied the score, and Manager Foster, evidently intending Coveleskie to stay in the box and take his medicine, let him remain on the slab. Finally Cove threw the ball at his feet and walked weeping out of the box. They never pitched Cove at my town again. Rather than pitch at Johnstown he would work a doubleheader the day before. Against other clubs Coveleskie was invincible; club after club would go down in shut-outs before his prowess, yet he could never defeat my team. One look at him from me would be like waving a red flag in a mad bull's face. He just could not work when I was around.

His grand showing in the Tri-State League that year led to his engagement with the Philadelphia club in the fall. It will be remembered that the Giants wound up their season with Philadelphia at the Polo grounds in New York. At the time they were but a few points in the rear of the Cubs of

Chicago, and the result of the race practically hinged upon the outcome of the Philadelphia-New York games. Coveleskie went in to pitch the first game with such speed and curves that he won with ease. Gotham fans wondered where he came from. After a day's rest Cove went into the box again, the result was the same, and the Phillies again defeated the pennant-aspiring Giants. But a slim chance for the pennant now remained for the frantic Giants, but Coveleskie went at them for his third game and down they went. With that game vanished all hopes of the pennant.

One would imagine that a pitcher who had performed such a great feat as Coveleskie would fairly set the League on fire the next season. Not so. Cove paid more attention to the coachers than he did to his work in the box and soon figured in a trade with the Cincinnati club. McGraw secured ample revenge at the Polo grounds in a game between the Giants and Cincinnati. When Cove was warming up to pitch, McGraw walked up to him and said, "Say, Cove, Ash is up in the stand with a ton of Cincinnati sausage. Look out for him." Poor Cove had evidently not forgotten me, for he broke all records in bases on balls that game and was sent to the Birmingham club of the Southern League. Manager McGraw said to me later, "Ash, I would have given $1,000 to have had you occupy a seat on our players' bench during the three games Cove pitched against us for Philadelphia." Now does it not seem strange that a man like Coveleskie should be afflicted with so strange a weakness? Your first thought will be, a lack of courage. Not so. I have seen Cove in a fistic encounter where he displayed more courage and staying power than he does in a game of ball when under fire. Coveleskie is unfortunate, indeed, in being so thin-skinned as to pay any attention to the wild ravings of the coacher. He is a perfect specimen of manhood, over six feet in height, possessing everything that a star pitcher should have, a gentleman at all times, and it's too bad that he and other thin-skinned players should allow coaching to drive them out of the major league. Were Coveleskie to ignore the coacher and pay the same attention to his work in the pitcher's box, he would be one of the greatest left-handers in the country today.

Queen City Graduates.

IT is doubtful if any city in the United States can boast of such an output of players as Cincinnati. Not only are the majors recruited from here, but I doubt if there is a minor league in the country that has not at least one Queen City representative. It was here in Cincinnati that the famous Buck Ewing graduated. On the lots of the town Ewing gradually developed into one of the greatest players in the profession. Amongst other old-timers may be mentioned Jake Stenzel, who led the National League in hitting one season, and Denny Lyons, of the Athletics, also a hitter of note. Shorty Fuller's work for New York is still doubtless remembered by old-time

Gotham fans. Long John Reilly, who for years held down first base for the Reds, is a native of the Queen City and still lives here. Jack Boyle developed into a crack catcher and then went to the four-time-champions, the old St. Louis Browns, where he became a star. Among other players who call Cincinnati their home, and whom old-timers will remember, are Bob Gilks, now doing scout duty for the Cleveland club, Harry Vaughn, Lefty Marr, Red Bitman, Bill Weidner, Ed Reeder, Johnnie Godar, Joe Straus, Bob Clark, Billy Clingman, Ed Boyle, Billy Klusman, Alex Voss and others.

Among latter day players, many of them still playing the game, are:

Miller Huggins, with St. Louis; Norman Elberfeld, with Washington; Bill Sweeney, with Boston; Jack Pfiester, with Chicago; McGee, with the St. Louis Americans; Schweitzer, with the St. Louis Americans; Chas. Dooin, manager Philadelphia Club; Lester Bachman, with the St. Louis Nationals; Pitcher Golden, with St. Louis Nationals; Nick Altrock, formerly with the White Sox; Lee Tannehill, with the White Sox; Jesse Tannehill, formerly with Pittsburg and Boston; Mike Kahoe, now scouting for Washington; Jack Thoney, formerly with the Boston Americans; George Schlei, now with the New York Giants; Bill Bartley, formerly with Athletics; Harry Armbruster, formerly with Athletics; Chas. Armbruster, formerly with Boston Americans; Orville Woodruff, formerly with Cincinnati; George Rohe, formerly with White Sox; Jack Sutthoff, formerly with Cincinnati; Jack Farrell, formerly with St.

Louis; George Yeager, formerly with Boston; Catcher Crist, lately with Philadelphia; Billy Hart, for years in the major leagues; Lolla Myers, formerly with Brooklyn; Ambrose Puttman, formerly with New York Americans.

Among the lesser lights are:

George Helmund, of Syracuse; Chas. Dexter, formerly with New Orleans; Ed. Tiemeyer, with Syracuse; Bill Elwert, with Toledo; Harry Matthews, with Atlanta; Whitey Morse, with Macon; Lefty Geyer, with Youngstown; Ed McKernan, with Paris, Ky.; Doc. Wiseman, with Nashville; Red Valdois, Virginia League; Al. Decker, O. & P. League; Reddy Mack, manager in W. Va. League; Jimmie Barton, manager, Newcastle; Henry Deisel, Texas League; Jimmy Houselman; Gus Bonno, Western League; Al. Baschang, Kansas League; Jack Bushelman, with Louisville; George Hogriever, Wisconsin League; Joe Schrall, New York League; Jake Henn, South Atlantic League; McGrew, formerly Southern League; Joe Hennessy, Southern League; Wm. Kohnle, Michigan League; Heinie Bush, Virginia League; Eddie Kolb, Minor League manager; J. J. Grim, Minor League manager; E. J. Ransick, Minor League manager; Catcher Ryan, Birmingham; Jake Deisel, Texas League.

All the foregoing, at one time or another, developed their talents on the playing grounds of the Queen City Millcreek Bottoms. It was here, from Buck Ewing down to the present-day player, that the boys were picked up by various clubs. Many a tale can be told of this historic training ground. It was in an amateur game one Sunday that I received my initial reprimand from my manager. This chap's name was Crockoe, and he had a peculiar way of retaining his players and securing the best amateur talent in the town. He was a huckster, and would appear at the player's residence, make the player's parents a present of a bushel of potatoes or a pound of butter and then exact from them a promise that they would insist upon their boy playing with his club the coming Sunday. Crockoe had many peculiar ideas. One Sunday we were playing a rival club. There were no seats and the spectators were arranged around the entire field. Crockoe was playing left field and I was holding down center. Jimmie Chard, later with Atlanta, was in the box for us. The opposing team had two men on the bases. Chard had the ball. I looked over to left field, and saw that Crockoe had disappeared. I shouted to Pitcher Chard, who was about to deliver the ball. "Wait a minute," I yelled, and started over to locate the missing Crockoe. Out he came from behind the crowd. "Oh, you thick-head!" he hurled at me. "You'll never play with us again if you don't use your nut a little. Why, you fathead, here I am hiding in the crowd, the batsman looks out and fails to see me, he hits the ball out here, I sneak in from behind the crowd and nab it. No, you'll never make a great player."

In another contest there was a big German holding the indicator named Bimpy Boehlein. Bimpy was boss of the game all the way through and would hold the German players to all of his unique decisions. Crockoe was at the bat one day and Boehlein called what looked to be a bad strike. "One sch'trike," yelled Bimpy. "Two sch'trikes," yelled Bimpy. Crockoe said not a word, but certainly looked a lot. The pitcher wound up and shot the ball over. Crockoe ducked it. "T'ree sch'trikes, you're out," yelled Boehlein. "What am I out for?" said Crockoe. "You're out for dodging." "I did not dodge," said the furious Crockoe. "You lie!" "I am a liar, am I?" said Boehlein. "Well! you had better dodge now." With that he sailed into the surprised Crockoe and before the battle was over both Germans gave an excellent exhibition of dodgings Boehlein never tired of telling the boys of the day. when he played ball. There was an old oak tree in deep right field, and it gave him especial pleasure to tell of the day he hit the ball "clean over dat wooden tree in right field."

Queen City Moguls.

CINCINNATI not only boasts of its wonderful contribution of ball players to the profession, but it has produced at least half a dozen magnates who stand at the head in the entire baseball world. Garry Herrmann, now at the head of the National Commission, is a Cincinnati boy, born and bred, as is Ban Johnson, President of the American League and a member of the Commission. John E. Bruce, the Secretary of the Commission is a Cincinnati boy. Robert Hedges and C. J. McDiarmid, principal owners of the St. Louis American League club, both hail from Cincinnati, and, last but not least, the celebrated Charles W. Murphy, the owner of the Chicago Cubs, is a Cincinnati boy, with Mr. C. P. Taft, a brother of the President, a noted Cincinnatian. Charley Dooin, a Cincinnati boy, is manager of the Philadelphia National League club, and there are many others in the front ranks of Balldom.

Pals.

ACCIDENTS on the ball field are bound to occur. Fatalities, while they have been few and far between, nevertheless have taken place. I recall an incident in the latter eighties that was pathetic in the extreme. Two boy friends, schoolmates, had left their homes to join their respective clubs down in the sunny south. They were Lefty Marr, who will probably be remembered by old-time fans, and Louis Henke. Both of these boys resided in Cincinnati and were inseparable comrades. They left their homes, happy, big, strong athletes, little thinking what was to befall them before their season was a month old. It happened in a game in Atlanta. Marr, who was a powerful big fellow, had hit a ball to the infield. Henke was playing first base on the opposing team. The ball was fielded to first base to head off Marr, but was thrown wild directly into the fast approaching runner. Henke reached over to get the ball, but the fast-flying Marr, unable to stop himself, went pellmell into him. Down went both of these big fellows. Poor Henke, it was his last game. He never recovered consciousness. They brought his remains back to his home town, accompanied by one silent mourner, Marr. Although nearly a quarter of a century has elapsed since this sad fatality, Lefty Marr has never been able to stand the heartaches of this awful calamity, for he has never been seen in his boyhood town, since they laid away the body of his pal, Henke.

A Looking Glass Scrap.

ON the Syracuse club, for a number of years, played Joe Schrall, an outfielder, and Nap Shea, a catcher. These boys were bang-up good-natured chaps and great friends. In fact, they were roommates. In the heat of battle one afternoon they sailed into each other and the comic part of the affair was furnished by Manager Griffin, of the Syracuse club, in his efforts to stop the contest. Manager Griffin was on the bench on crutches with rheumatism, and his attempts to stop the fight were ludicrous to behold. He hopped around on one leg trying to part them, and when the participants were finally stopped, Griffin was so far away from his crutches that they had to carry him back to the bench. The two scrappers called off hostilities for the time being, threatening the dire things they would do to each other after the game. The players kept a close watch on them for fear they would renew the fight. Shea and Schrall, upon arriving at the hotel, went to their room. Schrall was the first to enter the room and stationed himself in front of a large looking glass with a bat on his shoulder. Shea followed him into the room and

CHARLES F. CARPENTER
President of the Tri-State League

took his position on the opposite side, sitting on the bed which was directly in front of another mirror. Shea carried a large heavy mask, ready to start on Schrall in event he assaulted him with the bat. In this position the two were found by their fellow-players, who had followed them fearing for their safety. The two scrappers looked so funny, each glaring into a mirror, while grasping an implement of battle, that the boys burst into roars of laughter. Their mirth was contagious, and the fighters finally got to laughing themselves. Ill-feeling melted away and the boys made up and shook hands.

Two Hustlers.

I ONCE had an argument with a newspaper man who was a very dear friend of mine. This happened early in the season and we kept on bickering like two children, the entire year. The season closed and we were still quarreling. I attended the meeting of the National League in New York the following winter and whom should I meet there but my old newspaper friend. Through mutual agreement we smoked the pipe of peace, much to the delight of another dear friend of mine, Silk O'Loughlin. "Sure," said Silk; " you should have done it long ago. I tell you, Ash, a little drop of ink has made nations think." This adage, coming from this celebrated Celt, has since then remained with me. I am always there with the glad hand to any members of the pencil-pushers' union. Long may they wave! In my twenty years of experience they have said many things that stung, but, where they handed me one article of adverse criticism, I always noted there were hundreds of bouquets. As an illustration, it gives me pleasure to mention in this volume the great work the Philadelphia *North American* is doing not only for the Tri-State League, and for Wilkesbarre and Scranton of the New York State League, but also for all the independent clubs in the vicinity of Philadelphia. Not only does this enterprising sheet devote pages to these small leagues, but ever since the existence of the Tri-State League it has sent out its eminent sporting editor, Mr. George M. Graham, and its famous cartoonist, Mr. Walter C. Hoban, to the various towns in the Tri-State League. When these two pilgrims on their yearly jaunts go to these cities, the fur certainly does fly. Their illustrated articles in their paper anent the doings of the clubs in the Tri-State League have not only been of exceptional value to this League, but have aroused intense interest throughout the surrounding country. Messrs. Graham and Hoban are most welcome visitors throughout Tri-State League circles, and their annual visit is followed by an immense demonstration in their Sunday issue, describing and illustrating the doings of the club that they may have been visiting during the week. The *North American* through these eminent artists has done more for minor league baseball throughout Pennsylvania and New Jersey than some metropolitan dailies have done for their major league club. They have done much to keep intact the Tri-State League by their work, which constantly keeps the interest aroused throughout the League. I want to say were other minor leagues accorded the same support as the *North American* has given the Tri-State League through its hustling and hard-working pilgrims, Messrs. Graham and Hoban, there would be fewer crashes among the small clubs throughout the country.

A Grand Record.

THERE have been some grand old veterans connected with the game in the past quarter of a century. Old Cap Anson and Orator James O'Rourke both have splendid records. Cy Young has pitched in the National and American Leagues for twenty years—a most commendable record, but I am going to tell you of a player who for over twenty-five years has been pitching in both the large and small leagues. It was away back in 1883 that a youngster on the Lincoln Park lots in Cincinnati was showing excellent promise on the pitching slab in amateur league circles. In 1884 the Union League was organized in opposition to the American Association. They picked up this youngster, who was none other than the afterwards famous Billy Hart, who to this day is pitching in the Southern League. The Union Club lasted just two weeks and Hart went with an independent club at Urbana, Ohio. The year 1885 found Hart with the Chattanooga club of the Southern League. Clubs in those days were not overstocked with pitchers, like the teams of the present day, which carry them by the dozen. They had but two pitchers—Tom (Toad) Ramsey and Hart. Ramsey was a man of very uncertain habits. He would disappear at times for a week when on his periodical sprees, and of course all the pitching would fall upon Hart's shoulders until Ramsey showed up again. Hart was frequently called upon to pitch an entire series of games. On one occasion he pitched a series of four games against a league club and won all four of them. Several times he pitched a series of three games against a club. Can you imagine what would happen if you were to ask a present-day pitcher to work in every game for a week? In 1886 Hart stuck to the Chattanooga club. When the League disbanded he went with the Athletics of Philadelphia, remaining with that club until June, 1887, when the Athletics sold him to the Lincoln, Neb., club of the Western League. He won twenty out of the twenty-two games he pitched out there and his fine work attracted the attention of the Cincinnati club, which secured him from the Lincoln team. During the season of 1888 Hart in mid-season injured his pitching arm and the Cincinnati club sent him on to Buffalo. Owing to the injury to his arm, Hart played the outfield, for he always was a hard hitter. In 1889-1890 he was with the Des Moines club of the Western League.

In 1891 he went to the Sioux City, Iowa, club and his fine work in the box won the pennant of the Western League for his club. His showing with Sioux City again secured him a position with the big fellows, for the Brooklyn club of the National League purchased him from Sioux City. However, ill-fortune again followed Hart into the big league, for in the latter part of that season he injured his arm to such an extent as to compel him to leave the Brooklyn club for home. Arriving home he determined to give his troublesome arm a much needed rest and he not only lay idle the balance of the season, but rested the entire season of 1893. In 1894 it was back to the minors again with Hart, who went once more to the Sioux City club. His fine work again won for them the pennant, and a position with the majors for himself, for the Pittsburg club secured him. At the close of the season of 1895 that club traded him to the St. Louis club for infielder Bones Ely. Hart remained with the St. Louis club in 1896-1897 and at the close of the 1897 season was traded back to the Pittsburg club for Pitcher Hughey. In 1898 Hart was traded to the Milwaukee club of the American Association for Outfielder Beaumont. The year 1899 found Hart with the Minneapolis club, and in 1900 and 1901 it was back to the majors, for Cleveland secured him from the Minneapolis club. After two years with Cleveland, Hart went back to the minors as manager and pitcher for the Peoria club of the Western League. In 1904 Hart pitched part of the season and finished as an umpire in the American Association. In 1905 he returned to the slab and pitched creditably for the Columbus, Ohio, club, winning twelve out of sixteen games. In 1906 Hart again changed clubs and pitched for Indianapolis. The three following years, 1907-1908-1909, he was with Little Rock, of the Southern League, that club having purchased him from Indianapolis. In 1910 Hart was transferred from Little Rock to Chattanooga, that club having purchased the Little Rock franchise. So Bill Hart after more than a quarter of a century's performance in leagues, both major and minor, by a strange coincidence is returned to the club with which he made his professional debut.

Hart's record is truly a wonderful one. His arm still retains the remarkable cunning that kept him in and out of the major leagues for over twenty-five years. "I have always taken good care of my arm," Hart said recently. "I feel as young as I did twenty years ago. I don't drink any intoxicants and don't use tobacco in any form. I think for endurance I can pitch with any pitcher in the country and put up a pretty good game at that."

Hart won a majority of his games with the Chattanooga club in 1910, and has several offers to continue on his wonderful career. Judging from the enthusiasm he displays it looks very much as if he will keep on the second lap of another twenty-five years of service. Out in Bond Hill, a very pretty suburb of Cincinnati, is a pretty homestead, a monument to Hart's long service on the diamond. Here Bill is surrounded by his family, and a welcome hand is always extended to all visitors, who delight in hearing Bill's tales of his long career on the greensward. Hart's great record should prove a living illustration to that class of players who imagine the game is one long matinee and do not look out for the future. Larry McLean, of the Cincinnati club, names this class, "The Night-Leaguers." It was only the marvelous physical condition of Hart that kept him in the game for over twenty-five years. Had he been a member of the "Night-League," his finish would have been chronicled long ago.

A Marriage on the Diamond.

WE have heard of marriages on the stage, in the lions' den and at circuses, but it was my lot to witness a wedding on the diamond. The marriage took place in the early nineties at the Cincinnati ball grounds. Frank Bancroft, who has enjoyed a long and honorable career as business manager of the Reds, and still holds down that position, pulled off the affair. Business was bad that season and Bancroft, ever striving to increase the attendance, hit upon this scheme. But to find the candidates worried him not a little. At the park that year, assisting the superintendent of the grounds, was a happy-go-lucky pair of individuals who were known as the Can Brothers. One of them answered to the cognomen of Snooks, and the other, a big fat chap, sailed under the unique title of "Lollie-gah-plootz." Bancroft's wants became known to said Snooks, who lost no time in rushing to his pal Lollie. "Here, Lollie, I hear you are going to hitch up in a short time. Why don't you see Banny and have the marriage take place on the diamond?" This seemed to strike Lollie favorably, and no time was lost in arranging affairs with Bancroft, on condition that it would be satisfactory to his intended bride. Her consent was readily gained and Manager Bancroft was happy. The marriage was extensively advertised, in conjunction with a game that was scheduled with Baltimore. The ceremony was indeed an impressive affair. The couple met down in left-field at the club house, and marched up to the home-plate. Arriving there, both teams gathered in a semicircle around the happy pair. Following the couple on their way to the plate was Colonel Snooks, the other member of the Can Brothers, who acted as best man, and a large moving van carrying presents from the couple's friends. The stands were crowded with women. It seemed that every woman from the German districts of Cincinnati was on hand to witness Lollie's marriage. With both teams surrounding the couple the ceremony was soon performed without incident, except that Colonel Snooks tried to kiss the bride and narrowly missed creating a riot. Members of both teams congratulated the happy bride and groom and presented them with a liberal wedding gift. Bancroft agreeably surprised the couple with a complete household outfit, while "Lollie-gah-plootz" smilingly led his bride from the field amidst the cheers of the crowd.

Groundkeeper a Contract Jumper.

THAT genial old Celt, Mike J. Finn, who for years was at the head of the Little Rock club of the Southern League, was very much worried one day when he received a message from his people in Little Rock stating that his groundkeeper Murphy had disappeared. Finn and his club made the circuit of the league and arrived at Shreveport. At the grounds whom should Mike behold but his fugitive groundkeeper Murphy. Mike was furious. Bob Gilks, then manager of Shreveport, had induced

HUMOR AMONG THE MINORS

Murphy to jump Little Rock. Finn was very sore, for Murphy was a capable man and he threatened, "By t'under, at the nixt meeting, I shall have the ground t'inders reserved."

In 1901, I had a big darky at Newport News, Va., who was attending to my park. Barney was his name, and on numerous occasions I would be called upon to go down to police headquarters and pay a fine for the darky for some minor offense. One morning Barney failed to show up at the grounds and I, as usual, knew where to find him. I arrived at the station and there was Barney behind the bars. "So glad to see yous, Mister Eddie," was Barney's first greeting. "Please, sah, get me out just this once moh, and hurry up, so I can get de grounds ready." I inquired as to the reason of his arrest. "Didn't do a thing, Mister Eddie. I was at de Hell's Acre last eve'ng and I asked some fool nigger fo a dollah. Just because he didn't gimme de dollah, I bust him over de chops and took foh dollahs from de fool, and told him I maybe gib it back to him. Just then along come Captain Palmer and say, 'Bahney, you go along wid me.' I go along and heah I is. Best hurry up and get me out'en yer, if you wants to play today." I inquired from the authorities as to the charge against Barney and it was highway robbery. Barney did not accompany me out of jail that day, as he did on numerous other occasions, for he was presented with a ten years' sentence in State's Prison. I often think that had Mike Finn put through his resolution to reserve groundkeepers, Barney might have escaped his fate.

A Narrow Escape From a Fine.

GEORGE, or King Kelly, as he is better known in Virginia League circles, was a unique and witty character. The King hailed from Washington, D. C., was quite a comedian, and managed clubs in the Virginia and North Carolina Leagues for a number of years. His one great specialty when playing the outfield was, when a ball was hit in his direction, to turn his back while in pursuit of it. Just as it was descending, he would seize the ball, and the audience and batsman were unable to see whether Kelly had caught the ball or not, as Kelly had his back to them. Kelly would act as if he had actually dropped the ball. The crowd would naturally yell at Kelly's supposed error and the country batsman would keep on dashing around the bases. When he would arrive at second Kelly would throw in the ball, much to the discomfiture of the batter.

Kelly discovered Frank Smith, who for the past few years has done great work in the pitcher's box for the White Sox of Chicago. Kelly signed Smith at the magnificent salary of $50.00 per month, for his Raleigh, N. C., club. One day Smith failed to show up for practice and Kelly was wild. He threatened all sorts of dire things for Smith. A few days later Smith put in his appearance at the grounds, and Kelly seemed pacified.

A day or so after this incident Kelly read in a northern paper that Connie Mack had suspended Rube Waddell for insubordination. Kelly showed me the newspaper article and said, "Do you know,

Ash, I would have fined that Smith for the same thing the other day, but I couldn't think of the daggone word."

Utility Players.

IT is not an infrequent occurrence that members of the animal kingdom cut a figure in the outcome of the game. Abner Powell, who for years was most successful as owner, player, and manager of clubs in the south, once lost a game for his club when a lusty bull-terrier grabbed him by the seat of his trousers just as he turned to chase a ball that had been hit over his head. Powell might have caught the ball had not the terrier seized him and held on for dear life. By the time they had shaken the dog off, the batsman had scored with what proved to be the deciding run.

Outfielder Ralph McBride, who graduated from the Austin, Tex., club to the Cincinnati club in 1895, lost a game for his team at Austin in a most peculiar manner. One day a batsman hit a ball out to the fence and McBride gave chase. When he reached the ball he turned around without picking it up and ran toward the infield, apparently frightened out of his wits. The hit probably would have been good for two bases, but it rolled into the midst of a colony of lizards or chameleons. These little animals are perfectly harmless, but McBride, being a northern man, had never seen the little creatures of changeable colors. His failure to recover the ball gave the batsman a home run and the game.

The ballgrounds in the city of Johnstown are located on a place called the "Point," so named because two streams meet directly at the "point." Should a ball be hit foul over the grandstand it will land in one of the streams. Naturally, the loss of all these balls would have meant a great expense to the club-owners, were it not for the fact that they had an intelligent little water-spaniel to recover the balls. This utility fellow is chained to a spot **directly** in the rear of the stand and he has advanced to such a degree of intelligence that the moment he hears the umpire yell "foul," or even when he hears the ball tip the bat, he is tugging at his chains. The moment he is released, he is in pursuit of the ball. He will dive off the high embankment into the stream and it is a matter of but a few minutes before the ball is recovered. He is under salary to the Johnstown club and receives one dollar per game.

The Tri-State League was the first minor league that adopted and adhered to a strict salary limit. Altoona and Johnstown are intense rivals in that league, and some wag in Altoona caused the Johnstown club much annoyance by preferring charges against them for an alleged violation of the salary rule, by carrying an extra player, the dog, on the salary list.

Jiggs Donohue, the ex-White Sox first-baseman, while a member of the Dayton club for a number of years in the nineties, was the owner of a little monkey which indirectly won a game for his club one day. In some way this little monk secured possession of the visiting club's catcher's glove. With it he ran to the home bench and sat on it. He was a vicious little fellow and no amount of urging and persuasion could remove Mr. Monk from the glove. The catcher finally borrowed another glove, which he could not handle as well as his own, and a couple of balls got away from him that he claimed he would have caught with his own glove, thus losing a close game.

A Baseball Scout's Report.

DAD CLARKE, well known as a pitcher for the New York Giants, was once sent on a mission for a left-handed pitcher that his club had heard glowing reports about. Great stories were told of this coming southpaw. He had a curve like a wagon wheel, terrific speed, etc., and it was finally decided to send Clarke on to have a look at the wonder. Clarke arrived at his destination and lost no time in hunting up the phenom. One look at the wonder in action was enough for Clarke. The southpaw absolutely had nothing at all in his pitching repertoire. He had not enough speed to dent a pound of butter. Clarke took the first train back to New York. Meeting his manager he was plied with questions as to the ability of the much-heralded southpaw. "Did you see him? Did you see him pitch? How did he look?" "How did he look?" snorted back the disgusted Clarke. "Why, I'll tell you how the yap looked. Why, he looked like a right-handed pitcher with a sore arm."

HUMOR AMONG THE MINORS

A Slugging Match.

DOWN in Texas in 1895 I was a member of Ted Sullivan's Texas Steers. This team won the pennant hands down, and the scores by which they won ran up quite often into the double figures. We were playing the Houston Club one day and batted their pitchers all over the lot. Runs were coming over the plate fast and furiously. On the Houston club, playing first base, was a big good-natured German from St. Louis, named Charley Krehmeier. With the score about 18 or 20 to 2, I asked Charley, "What is the correct score, do you know?" "You blamed fool, Ash, how in the deuce should I know? The scorekeeper jumped the fence an hour ago."

The Grandstand Comedian.

DID you ever sit close to the loud-mouthed donkey in the grandstand whose delight it is to nag the visiting players, and to fill with disgust all those who are within hearing distance of his braying? This fellow can get away with his chatter in the major leagues, but in the minors, NEVER. I always take especial delight in silencing Mr. Donkey. You will notice him as soon as the game starts, for he likes to hear himself talk. The minute I take my place on the coaching lines he is after me. "Well, well, look who's here. Ash, are you still in the game?

Why, you played ball when James R. Garfield was shot." This creates a laugh at my expense. I join in the laugh and the crowd is with me. My team gets away to a bad start, the home club scoring a couple of runs, and Donkey is roaring with delight. "Mind the year you led the American Association at St. Paul in old age, Ash?" he roars. Another laugh, in which I join and the crowd is now with me strong, for Donkey has failed to rattle me. Finally I spy my tormentor in the stand, a benevolent-looking old chap with a beautiful assortment of whiskers, adorning his chin. From the way he is now carrying on, he seems to be sure of his ground. "Oh, Ash," he roars, "where did you get that bunch of misfits? Last place for you, sure. What will become of you? Where you going next season?" "To pieces," I retort, and the laugh is on his whiskers. My club ties the score. Donkey is strangely silent. My turn has now come. He is after me now only in a half-hearted manner. "Well, of all the lucky stiffs, Ash, to tie our club!" he yells as a last attack, when I get after him for fair. "Here, you," I yell, "don't you get tired of hearing yourself talk? I get paid for this stuff, so I have it on you. As for your whiskers, you will have to do one thing or the other, get shaved, or get some insect powder." The last I see of my tormentor, he is beating a hasty retreat out of the stand. "There goes Donkey for the insect powder," is my parting shot.

Slats Davis, the well-known umpire, was a past-master in getting back at obstreperous rooters. One day in Los Angeles, he put the quietus on a thin, sickly-looking little chap who had been joshing him.

After locating his man in the crowd, Davis in a polite manner asked the little fellow to stand up. Much to Davis' delight, he did so. "Now, take off your hat, little one." As he took off his hat, Davis convulsed everybody with laughter by saying, "That will do, Chauncey. Sit down. If you had a rubber on your head, you would look like a lead pencil." On another occasion in San Francisco he ran a henpecked rooter, who had been tormenting him, out of the grandstand by telling him to go home and cook his wife's supper.

Nick Altrock.

WHAT American League fan does not know Nick Altrock, until the past year one of the premier southpaws of Comiskey's Chicago White Sox? Nick is a Cincinnati boy, born and bred, and in his boyhood days when not sewing shoes in a factory, was busy striking out ambitious batsmen. When the White Sox won the American League pennant in 1906, there was much rejoicing among Nick's friends in Cincinnati. When the world's series between the White Sox and the Cubs was announced the excitement among them was intense. Excursions to Chicago were run and it is safe to say that the Cincinnati delegation to Chicago numbered fully five hundred of Nick's friends. Conspicuous among them was Nick's venerable father, who was chaperoned by the writer. Nick's pater was fairly burning up with excitement. Among that crowd the old

JOHN McGRAW
Manager of the New York Giants

gentleman was the happiest, until it came bedtime. He had never left the Altrock home since his advent in this country from the old "Vaterland," and when we showed him to his sleeping berth on the train he balked like a stubborn mule. In fact, we had to back him into the berth as one would a horse into a stall. All night he kept us awake asking me, "Ash, are you sure my Nick meet me at dot drain in de morning?" Being assured that Nick would be on hand in the morning the old gentleman would remain quiet for an hour or so, then he would wake up another of our party, with the same inquiries.

I wish I could describe the old gentleman's feelings when he beheld his Nick on hand bright and early at the depot the next morning. And when Nick took his place on the pitching slab before that immense mob at the West Side Park for the opening game of the series that afternoon, the old man was white with excitement. Would his Nick win? Was this his Nick, his own boy, that faced this howling, maddening throng of 20,000 people? Sure it was. Were not Nick's Cincinnati friends in his vicinity howling like mad? When the game was over, and the crazy White Sox rooters had lifted Nick to their shoulders, it was then that the old man fully realized that his boy had won. "Be Gott!" shouted the old man, vainly trying to reach his boy. "Come on, Ash. Come on, boys, vee get a t'ousand dollars worth of beer right avay." And such celebrating as that crowd of Cincinnati fans did that night. Many Chicagoans are doubtless wondering to this day who the patriarchal-looking gentleman was who made so merry with the younger generation.

At the conclusion of the series the victorious White Sox took an extended barnstorming tour, after which the members returned to their respective homes for the winter. The word came that Nick Altrock, the Cincinnati boy who had won the opening game of the world's series, would reach home on a certain day. Ever since the White Sox's victory over the Cubs there had been preparations going on to give Nick a welcome home that he would never forget.

The night for Nick's arrival home duly came. The committee in charge had not overlooked anything. There was a parade that beggared description, with automobiles, bicycles, wagons, and fully fifty carriages. All the shoemakers in Cincinnati seemed to be in that parade to welcome their fellow-workman home. In fact, the parade contained all classes from statesmen to brakemen. The procession proceeded on its way to the depot without incident. Nick arrived in due time with the bands playing a welcome and Nick smiling until his mouth looked like a torn pocket. Altrock was seized by his friends, seated in an automobile with his waiting father and escorted homeward by his admiring friends. The parade had advanced but a short distance from the depot when fireworks belched forth from every window and housetop along the line. This was a surprise to me, for I, being on the reception committee, knew that we had not contracted for any fireworks. The majority of spectators on the sidewalk were negroes and I commenced to wonder how Nick had become so popular with the colored population of Cincinnati. However, the mystery soon became clear to the wondering committee, for, when our parade had proceeded a few blocks up the street, another parade met us coming from the other direction. It happened to be a colored political organization that was on its way to a meeting and all the fireworks were intended for the prospective candidate and not for Altrock. Nick does not know to this day who paid for the fireworks. Altrock was feted all winter by his friends, yet how fickle is fame. When the White Sox failed to land in the running the following season, Nick's friends wanted to send a city ash cart down to the depot instead of the brass band, autos and carriages.

A Two-Club League: A Sharp Trick.

WE all remember the twelve-club League of a few years ago, but few of our readers will ever recall a two-club league. Yet such an organization existed. In 1900 the Virginia League officials, to avoid the long railroad jumps to Roanoke and Lynchburg, put me in charge of a club at Hampton, Va., a little city on Chesapeake Bay. The entire league was financed by Capt. E. H. Cunningham, of Norfolk (now a sea pilot) and the late Capt. J. H. Brady, of Portsmouth, Va. This apparently indicates syndicate ball, but such was not the case. When one of the smaller cities would get into financial trouble, both of the captains would rush to its aid, rather than see their pet little league go to the wall. Two squarer or gamer sportsmen than Cunningham and Brady could not be found, and Virginia may well be proud to boast of them as its sons.

The little League drifted on until the first part of August, when it surely looked as if the end had come. Richmond, Petersburg, and Newport News had thrown up the sponge. That left only Captain Cunningham's club at Norfolk, Captain Brady's club at Portsmouth, and what was left of my club at Hampton. Did Cunningham and Brady quit? No, they had just started. The choice of my team was distributed evenly among Cunningham's and Brady's clubs, and Norfolk and Portsmouth (rival cities) went on with a fight to a finish for the last forty days. It is doubtful if we drew a hundred people per day to the games, yet we did not throw up the flag.

On the Norfolk club, as one of its pitchers, was the now famous Christy Mathewson, for years the pitching sensation of the New York Giants. Captain Cunningham was moving heaven and earth to sell Mathewson to some club. I implored the Cincinnati club to take Mathewson. Imagine the great Mathewson going begging. Finally the New York club undertook to take Mathewson on trial and was to pay Captain Cunningham the sum of $2,000.00 in event the pitcher made good. At the close of our "Twin League" season Mathewson was sent on to New York. He pitched a few games with fair success. The season closed and Captain Cunningham heard nothing from the New York club as to their intention of retaining Mathewson. In the spring of the following season along came a letter from N E. Young, then President of the National

League, stating that the Cincinnati club had drafted Mathewson from the Norfolk club, and inclosing the Cincinnati club's check for one hundred dollars ($100.00) which was our League's draft price. A short time later the New York club traded the once famous Amos Rusie to Cincinnati for Mathewson, whose great work has been since then the sensation of both major leagues. Wasn't that sharp practice for a president of the New York club to pull off? Cunningham and Brady had kept their little league together in hopes of recovering some of their losses through the sale of Mathewson. It looked as if they had fallen a prey to the sharp tactics of the New York president, but they kept on fighting, and it gives me particular pleasure to state that a few years later, the purchase price was paid over to them, through the efforts of John M. Ward, who after a rigid battle in the courts gained a decision in their favor.

Could Mike O'Connor Hit?

WAY back in 1895 I played center field for Ted Sullivan's Texas Steers at Dallas, Tex. It was the year that Corbett and Fitzsimmons, under the management of Dan Stuart, were to battle for the championship of the world at Dallas. The town was fairly fight-mad, and was flooded with fourth-rate fighters. Almost every saloon in Dallas had a ring pitched in the back yard. The new arena was being erected in the vicinity of our ball grounds, and some of the fighters did light work on our infield. One morning while at practice along came a fourth-rate fighter who sailed under the nom de plume of "The Kansas City Mouse," with his retinue of trainers, and attempted to take possession of our infield. At this time who happened along but Captain Mike O'Connor, who peaceably asked the "Mouse" to leave the diamond until we had had our morning practice. This did not appeal to the "Mouse" and he became abusive. "Why, you gray-haired old stiff," he said to O'Connor, "look out, protect yourself. When I count three I am going to hit you. One, two," started the "Mouse." Bing! out went O'Connor's right and down went the bluffer. "There, you can count eight hundred now," was all that O'Connor said.

Hard Luck.

WHAT do you think of a player getting six hits in one game and being released the same night? Yet this was an actual occurrence in a game at Grand Rapids, Mich., in 1898. Joe Schrall, who was a hitter of the old school, joined the Grand Rapids team, which was owned and managed by Frank Torreyson of Pittsburg. That day, Schrall hit safely every time up. Toward the end of the game he got into a controversy with Manager Torreyson, who, notwithstanding Schrall's fine hitting, released him on the spot.

Worse Luck.

ON my champion team in 1906 I had a third baseman who was fired out of the game by me one day in a rather amusing manner. During a game at Scranton he made one of the most wonderful one-hand stops that I had ever seen. In making the stop the force of the ball whirled him almost off his legs. While in this position, and way off his balance, instead of throwing to first base, he threw the ball into left field. It was not until then that his condition dawned upon me. He had had a bad time the night before and was enjoying a beautiful jag. "Get out of here," I said. "What do you mean by coming on the field in this condition?" Out he went, muttering that I was the blankety-blankest manager he ever saw, putting a fellow out of the game for making a one-handed stop.

No Hair.

IN the old days the majority of players always wore mustaches. Nowadays there are at least a couple of players who go the old-timers a few better by wearing toupees. There is a well-known minor league pitcher who is very fussy about adorning his bald top-piece, wearing two different wigs, one for the game and the other for street wear. This fellow had the misfortune to meet with an accident to one of his legs at Holyoke a short time ago, and was compelled to use crutches. On a rather windy day he was on a street corner chatting with a young lady, when along came a gust of wind, blowing off not only his hat, but also his toupee. Forgetting for the moment his injured leg, he dropped his crutches and gave chase to his wig and hat. He broke all records recovering them. This player was noted for being out of the game on the slightest pretext, and when his manager heard of the trick the wind had played on him, he released him outright, as he had long suspected the player's injuries were not as serious as he claimed.

Another time at Cincinnati, the Reds had a manager who was not overly blessed with hair on his head. One day he was playing first base in a game at Cincinnati, when one of his infielders made a wild throw to him at first base. The ball went away over his head and as he gave chase to recover the ball, the wind blew his cap off. Instead of continuing to chase the ball, he now gave chase to his cap. By the time he recovered the headgear a couple of runners had scored, and with them went the game to the visitors.

The Umpire Never Wrong.

YOU can never make an umpire admit that he was wrong. He will never admit it to any player. Tim O'Rourke, the old-time second baseman of the early nineties, who gained fame later by being traded from Baltimore to Louisville by the now-famed manager, Hughey Jennings, was a member of the New Castle, Pa., club in 1899. O'Rourke had the misfortune to get hit in the throat with a pitched ball, which injured his vocal chords to such an extent that he could scarcely speak above a whisper, and was afterwards known as "Voiceless Tim." In a game at New Castle one day, Bud Lally was umpiring, and was away off on balls and strikes. "Get them over," we would yell from the bench. "Ten dollars fine for you, O'Rourke," yelled Lally to us on the bench, "I'll keep you quiet." O'Rourke was furious. He could not be heard ten feet if he yelled his head off, still Lally maintained that he was not wrong. You can't beat the umpire.

The Crab.

HAVE you ever noticed the surly, sulky-looking individual who, when he fails to make a hit while at bat, throws his stick up against the stand, and makes his way snarling and barking at everybody back to the player's bench? This individual, dear reader, is, in baseball parlance, known as the "crab." Nothing that is done in the game, in his estimation, was the proper thing to do. He is never wrong, always right. He is really a harmless individual and should be accorded pity instead of censure. One might apply to him the old adage, "He that cannot be counseled, cannot be helped." Mr. Crab starts his work early in the spring, when the players are ordered out for their daily morning practice. "Well, well," he will commence, "a guy like me in a Sarsaparilla League like this!

Hitting 300 and am asked to come out here for morning practice. Why, this skull of a manager of ours actually smuggled me out of the big show. Here I am, and I got the opposing outfielders in this League bowlegged chasing my drives. Of course my old soupbone (throwing arm) is not as strong as it used to be, but if I had about twenty pounds off my kitchen (stomach), I would show this yap manager he made a mistake in sending me down here in the jungles. And the mutt we are working for now! Why, my last year's manager forgot more baseball than this load of hay of ours ever knew. It's back to the big show for me, enough of the jungles. What do you think of him telling me the other day when I happened to fan with the bases full, that I could not hit the water if I fell overboard when there were men on the bases? Then the idea of telling me to sacrifice. Why, it's a crime to even ask a hitter like me to hit and run."

In the game, if Crab gets a base hit the first time at bat, well and good; but suppose he goes out on an easy chance. Then the air is black and blue with his vaporings. "Well," he roars, when he sees who is in the box for his club, "no wonder I ain't hitting, with this jinks pitching for us. That manager of ours certainly uses swell judgment in selecting his pitchers." Then to the pitcher, "I never could hit behind you. If you'd pitch for us every day I would wind up the season with a batting average of 000." The pitcher now gives a base on balls and a couple of hits follow. "Well, of all the morning practice pitchers, you are the limit. Get them over the plate, what's the matter with you? Is the plate in the ocean or are you in a rocking chair? I think you are handing the manager something or he would have derricked you an hour ago. Why, you couldn't pitch hay for me."

At this juncture a fly ball goes into the air to Mr. Crab. " I got it," he loudly yells. Down comes the ball and Crab drops it. It's now utterly impossible to see ten feet from Crab, owing to the language that he is belching forth. "Why don't this manager of ours have this ground fixed? And them cheap stiffs of club-owners, why don't they loosen up and buy a ball grounds?" The game is now over, his team won, and one would imagine the crabbing had ceased. Not on your life, it has only commenced.

"Of all the lucky stiffs, this manager of ours takes the cheese. Why, this pitcher had nothing in the box today but a prayer and wins his game. A guy with any brains would have yanked him out. Yesterday he yanks a guy out for hitting a couple of fellows and walking five more in succession. Why, that mutt couldn't manage a dog fight for me. Brains? Why, if our manager's brains were composed of dynamite and some guy would apply a lighted match to them, there would not even be a puff, let alone a report."

The club is off for a series of games on the road. "What time do we pull out, Mr. Manager?" queries Crab. "Eight o'clock tonight. Be on hand early; lots will be drawn for sleeping car berths, as there is only a limited number of lowers." The Crab is on hand at train-time, and makes his drawing for a berth, and draws an upper. He rushes to the manager. "Here you, no upper berth for me. Me sleeping in a peach tree and some fellows on this club that have not made a base hit since I was a kid, sleeping in the lowers? Not for me, I'll go home on the first train." Did Crab go home? You could not drive him home with a revolver. The next morning he is handed a dollar for his breakfast, and into the dining car he wanders. The waiter has met him before and is anything but pleased to serve him. "A couple of boiled eggs and some coffee for me," he says to the waiter. The morning meal being disposed of, he pays his bill of twenty-five cents and pockets the seventy-five cents change. Did he tip the waiter? Yes, he did not.

The club has now arrived at its destination and the players are assigned to their respective rooms at the hotel. Presently there is an awful roar from Crab. "What, me sleep in that dump? Why, the room is more like a freight car." However, Crab is finally pacified and hies his way down to the dining room for his dinner. "Soup and fish for mine," orders Crab from the waiter. The dishes are duly served and the soup gets into instant disfavor with Crab. "Here, waiter," he shouts, "take this varnish back to the kitchen and tell the chef if I want any inside painting done, I will more likely have it done by a painter. I'll not stand for your serving out such stuff and calling it soup. Bring me some roast beef, corn beef and cabbage, fricassee of chicken and a full line of vegetables." The waiter rushes off to the kitchen and arrives in due time. "Whow, look at this roast beef, fellows; why, it isn't as large as my watch charm. Is it any wonder I am falling off in my hitting?" Crab goes through the meal in a most artistic manner, not a morsel being left, and is presented with a bill for two dollars by the waiter. He signs it and it is duly settled for by the manager. Quite a difference in the price of the morning and noon meal, don't you think?

Crab is now not hitting so well. He is in the midst of a woful batting slump, and his actions are almost unbearable. "Why, them cheap club-owners are ringing in ten-cent balls on us. You couldn't shoot them out of the diamond with a Springfield rifle. They'll be compelling us to buy tickets at the gate next. The other fellows hitting, you say? Well, it's about time, at that. You talk about horseshoes, why, it's a shame to take some of them hits them guys is getting. That's just my luck. Of course I have been on two clubs this season before that mutt of ours got me, but it's back to the major leagues for me. I'm sick and tired of this Sarsaparilla League. Hello, what's this I see in the newspapers? A new man coming to replace me? Well, if this ain't the limit. That mutt of a manager has got the gall of a burglar to even think of replacing me. I'll have his job next season, see if I don't. If that mutt can fool them this long, what can a guy like me with brains do? What, that for me, boy?" addressing a messenger boy. "Yes," replied the lad. Crab opened the envelope and read as follows:

"You have been released to this club. Report at once.

"SWAMP ROOT BALL CLUB,
"Mosquito-Valley League."

Poor Crab has knocked himself out of the third position of the year. His manager has disposed of him to some far-off league, not wanting a man of Crab's disposition. Crab left for his new field of labor, vowing he would forsake even the big show and come back and show up his manager, who was so thick-headed as to release a player of his ability. But he never came back.

Some Comedian.

IN the old Inter-State League in the early nineties, there was a grand old second-baseman with the Fort Wayne club, Peck Sharpe. As a comedian he had them all tied to a post. One Sunday, Sharpe's club was playing at Dayton, Ohio. All the games are played there at Fairview Park. Adjoining the ball park was a summer resort. Among other attractions this resort had billed for that day, was a balloon ascension and parachute drop by a young lady. The ascension was made during the ball game. The balloon soared high up into the air, directly over the ball grounds, the parachute dropped and the girl landed directly on second base. Sharpe rushed to the young lady as she landed rather heavily on the ground, brushed off her dust-begrimed tights and exclaimed, "I am sorry for you, young lady; you made a great slide but the umpire says you are out."

At the same park one day the late Doggie Miller was having the time of his life joshing Lefty Geyer, the center-fielder of the Grand Rapids club. Geyer stood Miller's nagging for the biggest part of the game, when he finally turned on the kidder with the following: "Why, Doggie, you've got a good chance to keep quiet. You've been playing ball for twenty years, and have nothing to show for it but a sunburnt face." As Miller had always squandered his money as fast as he earned it, this was a telling shot, and he stayed off Geyer for the balance of the game.

Superstitions.

SOME of the superstitions that exist among ballplayers are ridiculous in the extreme. I will dwell upon only one. When I had charge of the Syracuse club one of my players rushed up to me, after I had shaken hands with a visiting player, and exclaimed, "Good heavens, Ash, don't shake hands with that jinks; why, we won't win another game this season!" "Oh, bosh," I declared, but no, my man insisted that our hopes for the pennant were from that time on blasted. I only laughed, but he went on: "Didn't I shake hands with him down in Baltimore, and I went right to bed sick that same day. Didn't Mike Joyce of Wilkesbarre borrow his glove, and Del Drake shook hands with him three weeks ago, and neither has made a base hit since? Pitcher McCloskey had his team 5 to 0 in the seventh inning when he borrows a chew of tobacco from jinks, and didn't they come in the following inning after that and clout McCloskey for six runs and the game? Didn't Jack Dunn of the Baltimore club carry him on his club for two years just to shake hands with the guy that was to pitch against his club that day?" My Syracuse club made a game fight for the pennant and would probably have landed the championship, had not my center fielder Goode been stricken with typhoid fever about ten days before the close of the season, and my chances for the pennant went glimmering. "Didn't I tell you that guy put the jinks on us when you shook hands with him?" yelled my superstitious player. No amount of argument could convince the superstitious one that jinks had not brought on Goode's illness, and lost the pennant for us.

An Indian Story.

SINCE the reign of Sockalexis, there have been few Indians to reach the major leagues. Chief Meyers of the Giants is the only one left. Pitcher LaRoy went to Boston from St. Paul, but but only for a limited stay. Jude, another Indian, went to the minors from Cincinnati, and is still hanging on at Lincoln, Neb., in the Western League. LaRoy was on my St. Paul club in 1907 and often regaled the boys with Indian tales. One day a member of the club approached LaRoy, asking him to decide a discussion. What he wanted to know was, if the city of Sheboygan, Wisconsin, was a Swedish or a French name. Both of the boys were sure they were right in their argument, and were willing to back their opinion with the ready cash. "Neither one of you boys is right," said LaRoy. "I will

CONNIE MACK
Manager of the World's Champion Athletics of Philadelphia.

tell you how the now grown-up city of Sheboygan received its name. In the early days of the red men there was a tribe of Indians traveling on their way to the north woods. They camped on the spot where the city is now located. During the encampment the squaw of the chief of the tribe presented him with a little son. The chief, who was a great man among the various tribes, was highly elated, as this was his seventh son. Whenever he was asked as to the sex of the little one, he would reply, 'She Boy Again.' When the tribe left the camp where the little one was born, he named the place "Sheboyagain." So that is how the little Indian camp grew into the prosperous little city of Sheboygan, Wisconsin." LaRoy is a highly intelligent member of his race, a graduate of Carlisle, and not in the habit of stringing anybody, so we accepted this story as the true version of the name's origin.

An Alias That Did Not Last Long.

ON my champion Scranton club of 1906 I had a young outfielder that Manager McGraw of the Giants was kind enough to send on to me for further development. Graham was not much of a batsman, but was chain lightning on the bases and in the outfield. He had some scruples about playing Sunday baseball, his father having strictly forbidden him to play on the Sabbath. My club was then a contender for the championship, and the fight promised to be a close one. I could ill afford to lose his services on the Sabbath, as we usually played a double-header on that day, so I prevailed upon him to play under an assumed name. Graham consented to this proposition and decided to play under the name of Wright. He was quite a fighter while in the game and his aggressiveness once led him into a fracas on a bright Sunday at Scranton when he and the umpire indulged in a battle of fisticuffs in the middle of the diamond. On another Sunday at Syracuse, Graham, alias Wright, had a glorious day at the bat. Out of four times up, he hit out a home run, two three-base-hits and a single. He was very much pleased at his big day's work, and after the fourth time at bat, he rushed wildly up to the press-box saying to the reporters, "Look here, boys, my name is not Wright today, it's Graham." Four hits killed off the alias.

Peculiar Playing Fields.

AFTER viewing the palatial playing grounds at Forbes Field, in Pittsburg, Shibe Park, in Philadelphia, the palace of the fans in Cincinnati, and other structures dedicated to the great national game, I cannot help but look back in the past at some of the shacks we poor minor leaguers were compelled to put up with. I remember at Rome, N. Y., there was a large "horse restaurant," as it had been named by the players, in right field. The diamond was situated at the county fair grounds and when the windows of the barn were open we played quite frequently to members of the equine tribe. In Troy, N. Y., the ballgrounds are situated on an island in the Hudson River. In left field there is a deep filling and a platform of heavy timbers that extends far out into the river. The same conditions exist in right field. When the fielder in pursuit of the ball reaches this wooden platform, it reminds one of a team of horses trotting over a rustic bridge.

In Tarboro, N. C., a tent is used to shield the athletes from the deadheads, a term, however, which is applied only to the colored population of this little North Carolina town, for woe betide the white citizen of the hamlet should he be seen in the neighborhood of the ballgrounds without handing his fee to the club officials. He would be drummed out of the town. In New Orleans, years ago, some wag said there were too many "dead balls," as there was a cemetery adjoining the field and frequently the balls were batted into the sacred grounds. In San Francisco, an obnoxious property-owner has an eyesore of a shanty in right-center, diagonally built, and collisions between the right and center fielders are not infrequent. In Wilkesbarre and Scranton the grounds are said to be undermined, and the latter field is surrounded by mountains of culm banks. The green grass diamond is quite a pleasant sight in contrast to these large dark piles. Galveston, Texas, and Atlantic City, N. J., have grounds that play havoc with the player's underpinning. They are situated on the beach, and the heavy sand is anything but favorable to the players. In Oswego, N. Y., the setting sun and the waves of Lake Ontario dazzle the batsman during the latter part of a game. The rays of Old Sol pour themselves into the lake on a direct line with the batsman, who for all the world imagines he is looking into a large mirror, making it utterly impossible to see the approaching ball. In the coal regions of Pennsylvania, at Pottsville and Shenandoah, the Sunday grounds are built on the top of Tumbling Run and a ridge of the Blue Mountains. They are most loyal fans in these two towns, for they are obliged to climb these mountains to view their favorite pastime. Nashville, Tenn., has a field built deep down in a valley. Right field is rather short and runs up to the fence on a sloping embankment. Right-fielder Wiseman of the Nashville club evidently has a lifelong position with that team, for the way he runs up on that embankment and seizes the long fly balls would remind one of a Rocky Mountain goat. Wiseman is familiar with every foot of ground on this embankment and he really has a decided advantage over the visiting fielder. He has been with the club ten years.

St. Paul's downtown park has long been the joke of American Association players. The park is so small that it has been dubbed, the "Cigar Box." Long telegraph poles encircle the entire grounds. On these, wire nettings are adjusted. In viewing your first game on these grounds you become imbued with the idea that there are ten men in the game. Right field is so short, that the second baseman plays his position directly over the second bag. The right-fielder, in the meantime, is compelled to play exactly where the second baseman would be playing on a regulation ground. Base-hits into right field are frequently scored as errors in event the right-fielder fails to throw a batter out on a hit into his territory. It is nothing unusual for any St. Paul outfielder to have an abundance of assists. The St. Paul club also has a Sunday grounds, outside the city, which is one of the largest in existence, thus owning the largest and smallest grounds in the country. When the St. Paul catchers were playing on the large grounds, they were at times so confused that they would not start in pursuit of a high foul ball, having become accustomed to the small grounds, where they were utterly unable to move out of their tracks owing to the limited territory they had to work in.

At Johnstown, Pa., in the Tri-State League, the grounds are the property of the city and have been donated as a children's playground. The youngsters are allowed the use of the grounds every day until 2 P. M., when they must vacate to allow the regular game to take place. The fence is portable, erected on large and heavy steel girders, and on the extreme ends of the park there are two large barns, into which the fence is immediately slid on rollers after the game, and the ground is again in possession of the youngsters. I often wonder what some of our present day stars would say were they obliged to play on any of these brush grounds.

Dear Old O'irland.

HARRY VAUGHN, the ex-Cincinnati catcher, after he left the major leagues, had a most prosperous career as manager of the Birmingham, Ala., club of the Southern League. Harry won a couple of pennants for the Iron City and made quite an enviable record for himself in Dixie. On

Vaughn's team one year was a big husky Celt by the name of Patrick Millerick. Pat was not only a first-class catcher but he was a great stickler for his native heath. It was Ireland first, last, and all the time with Millerick. His love for the "Ould Sod" led him into quite a controversy with his manager one night in front of a Birmingham hotel. After very little argument Pat's enormous right swung out, landing full upon Vaughn's jaw. Down went the manager in a heap. The crowd instantly gathered and seized Pat. "Here, Pat," some one asked him, "what did you want to strike your manager for? Too bad you should so forget yourself as to hit your manager." "Shure, shure, too bad I didn't kill the baste, but I had to hit the h'athen. He said Texas wor bigger than O'irland."

A Bad Actor.

ONCE in a while managers of ball clubs run across obstreperous players who are exceedingly hard to handle. I had one of these chaps on my club while at Shreveport in the Southern League. This fellow's name was Childs, and he was not a half-bad chap when not in his cups. When he was drinking he was a terror. I got tired running around the block with Childs and a knife after me, so I palmed him off on my dear old friend Mickey Finn, who was running the Toledo club of the American Association. At first Childs refused absolutely to report to Finn. Mike wired him to come on to

Toledo at once, stating there would be no trouble in coming to terms. Childs finally decided to report, and arrived safely at Toledo. Finn and the bad one got together and Finn made him a rather liberal proposition as to salary, but Childs could not see it. "I want 'thee' (3) 'undred dollars ah month, or nothen," said Childs in a rich southern dialect. But Finn would not accede to this demand. "Well, then, tell me, sah, why won't you give me thee 'undred dollas a month?" demanded Childs. "Well, I'll be frank with you, Mr. Childs; it's because you are not worth it," replied Finn. Bing, went the southerner's big fist on the unsuspecting Finn's jaw. It's useless to add that Finn sent the bad one back to me on the first train. Later in 1904 I received a letter from Childs' venerable father down in Georgia stating it was his firm belief that his boy had ceased using intoxicants, and begging for another opportunity on my club. The old gentleman's pleadings were so sincere that I told him to send the boy on to me at Charleston. I am glad to state that the old gentleman's statement proved correct. Childs did not drink a drop and did great work for me. I once asked Childs why he did not abstain from drink while he was with me at Shreveport, and had a chance for advancement into a major league. He said, "I'll tell you, sah, Mr. Eddie. When I lef' Georgia and de ole folks, I promised Dad I would not touch any licker, as de ole man tole me that if Mr. Ashenback sent me back again for drinking, he would shore kill ma'h, sah." Childs had wonderful ability for a youngster, but grew to such proportions that his immense size gradually drove him out of the game.

My dear old friend, Tim Murnane, the dean of Boston's baseball authorities, has often told a tale of my inclosing the release of Childs in a tin can, and dropping it down to the player from an upper floor of a Little Rock hotel. Not guilty, Tim.

Arguments With Kelly.

HAILING from the coal regions is a big sunny old Celt, called "Shamokin Mope-up Kelly," who has been umpiring in various leagues for the past twenty years. Throughout the country he is known familiarly as "Mope Up Kelly." When the players show a tendency to loaf during the game, you will hear Kelly yell, "Mope Up, Byes, Mope Up," hence his sobriquet. In the tail-end of the year of 1902 I had the Shreveport club of the Southern League and in a game at New Orleans, Kelly officiated. He had a particularly hard game that day, and the players cussed him black and blue. Kelly evidently knew he was off, for usually he was very strict in discipline and would not stand for any back talk, but this time he met the verbal attacks with a bland, sunny smile. Finally, in about the seventh inning, my pitcher came walking back to the bench, stating that Kelly, who was working in the middle of the diamond, had ejected him from the game. This was a surprise to me as there was apparently no sign of a "chewing match" between Kelly and my pitcher. I rushed out to Kelly, demanding to know why he had put out the pitcher, and had let the New Orleans players cuss him all through the game. "Why," said I to Kelly, "my man was never known to use profanity in all his life." "That may be true, Ash," replied Kelly, "but the big town bum told me I had been to mass Sunday, had put a dime into the contribution box, and then had taken out ninety cents. I'll have 'im suspinded for this."

In Wilkesbarre one day Kelly was officiating. After the game he passed the City Hall. "Who won the game, Kelly?" asked a policeman. "Wilkesbarre, 2 to 1," was the response. "Did Pete Noonan do anything?" the copper asked. "He did," said Kelly; "I called a third strike on him and he called me an Irish liar."

Corcoran's Quick Wit.

ONE of the wittiest gentlemen it has been my pleasure to meet was Tom Corcoran, for years the great shortstop of the Cincinnati club. I will never forget the hot one he put over on Dan Kerwin at the Cincinnati club's training quarters in Dallas, Texas. Joe Kelley was in charge of the Redlegs at that time, and upon Kerwin's arrival at Dallas, Kelley immediately took him in tow and introduced him to his fellow club-members. Among those whom he met was Corcoran. "Here," said Kelley, "Dan, meet Mr. Corcoran, who will be your captain the coming season." "Oh," said Kerwin, in a patronizing way, "I know Tommy Corcoran all right. Why, he used to take me into the game when I was a boy." "I did, did I?" responded Corcoran. "Well, if I did, I took you in by the whiskers."

Heredity.

MICKEY CORCORAN, the infielder the Cincinnati club purchased from Buffalo recently, was playing for a number of years in the Eastern League. Corcoran is a Buffalo boy, and his parents were regular visitors to the games in his home city. His venerable mother, on one of his first visits to Buffalo, was very anxious to know how her boy was doing, so she hunted up Corcoran's manager and asked, "Shure, and how is my boy Mickey getting on?" On being informed that Mickey was about as good as there was in the League, she proudly replied, "Faith, it's only natural that my Mickey is a grand player. Faith, warn't his fayther the best handball player in O'irland?"

Too Anxious.

OUT on the Pacific Coast some years ago, Jack Grim won a hard-fought championship for Portland, Ore. He had as one of his catchers a hustling young Celt named Shea. It used to be the practice for the player who had the last put-out to keep the ball. Shea's anxiety to get the coveted sphere lost a game for his club at Spokane one day. There were two Spokane men on the bases, second and third, respectively, one out, and a base hit would win the game for Spokane. The next batsman struck out and Shea, with a wild yell, put the ball in his hip pocket and made a dash for the bus, thinking it was the third out. He did not run far, as the men on the bench seized him, frantically yelling that there were only two out and trying to get the ball out of his pocket. Alas, for poor Shea! by the time they got hold of the ball the two baserunners had scored and the game went to Spokane. In later years Shea, who was a native of California, and was not of a saving nature, came near being disowned by the elder Shea. Arriving home from his disastrous Eastern trip he rang the paternal doorbell and was met on the threshold by his father, who flew into a rage when he saw the prodigal son. "It's you, is it, Dinnie?" said he. "Well, be off wid yez; who the hell ever heard of a Shea coming home on Christmas wid a straw hat on."

A Kind Heart.

GEORGE ENGEL, the Cincinnati boy, who for the past six years has been out on the Pacific Coast, tells a funny one on John J. McCloskey, late manager of the St. Louis club. Several years ago McCloskey's club was playing a game at Portland, Ore. On his team he had a player named Thielman who attempted to get gay with his manager. Anybody who is acquainted with McCloskey knows that there could be but one result and poor Thielman, after a game fight, was a badly beaten man. Engel, in telling of the battle says, "While Thielman lost the battle, you have got to hand it to McCloskey, for he sent Thielman to the best hospital in Portland."

German Rooters.

DURING my twenty years' experience in baseball I have noticed that the German rooter is the most original and amusing one. Milwaukee, Reading and Lancaster are where the German rooter predominates. My St. Paul club played a series of games in 1907 at Milwaukee with Perry Werden acting as umpire. As is customary, Werden announced the batteries before the game. "LaRoy and Sugden will be the battery for St. Paul. Curtis and Roth for Milwaukee." "Who's dot vat iss going to pitch?" came a voice from behind a big bottle of beer in the rathskeller underneath the grandstand. "Why, Christy Mathewson," said Werden, in a joshing way. "De devil you say!" retorted the voice. "Vat time did he get in Milwaukee?"

In Reading, Pa., dwells a German rooter who became so enthusiastic over the showing of his home team that he threatened to take all comers on wagers that his favorite club would win the next four out of three games. In Lancaster that club beat my Altoona club out of the pennant in 1909. On the last trip to Lancaster a big German from his seat in the bleachers begged and implored me not to take "Green Paris" over the loss of the pennant.

Another German rooter in Milwaukee on a rainy day brushed by an attache of the ball park who was distributing rain checks at the gate as the patrons passed into the park. "Here, sport," shouted the gatekeeper to our German friend, "you have forgotten your rain check." "To h—l mit your raincheck!" shouted back the German; "I got me an umbrella."

In 1907 Jack Doyle had charge of the Milwaukee club and made a great fight for the pennant, while my St. Paul club was a hopeless last. Notwithstanding the great showing made by Doyle, the Germans were loud in their demands that I be secured as manager. "We vant Ashenback. He iss one of our beoples. Let Doyle go to Louisville."

Poetic Coaching.

THE coal regions of Pennsylvania have contributed their share of ballplayers to the profession. In the Lackawanna Valley, within a radius of a few miles, lie the thriving mining towns of Scranton and Wilkesbarre, and quite a formidable team could be selected from their sons. From Avoca, a suburb of Scranton, hails the now famous manager of the Detroit Tigers. Bill Coughlin, his able captain when they fought so valiantly for the world's championship, resides in Scranton, as does Jack Dunn, the clever manager of the Baltimore club. Piggy Ward and the O'Neil boys, Jack and Mike, once famous as a battery, reside in Scranton also. Factoryville, a short distance away on the trolley, claims the peerless Christy Mathewson as its own, while along the Valley reside Buck Freeman, who can still hit them out; Jimmie Mullen of Newark; Mike Konnick, of the Cincinnati club; McCabe, formerly of the same club; Steamer Flanagan and other lesser lights.

I well remember catcher O'Neil's debut as a professional. Hank Ramsey engaged him for his Courtland club of the New York State League. O'Neil was a strong husky Irishman, working in the mines, before Ramsey signed him up, and was green as grass. Ramsey sent him out to coach one day on the third base line, and O'Neil convulsed everybody on the grounds with his rich Irish brogue. With a runner on second and third, O'Neil, who had never coached before, yelled, "Eehr yeez are, and there yeez go! Now may the both of yee come home on the same blow."

The Sport of Kings.

THE ponies appeal more or less to members of professional balldom. Not that all players take a shy at the runners, but it is a safe wager that a majority of the profession have a warm spot in their heart for the races. Among those who always are ready to back their judgment on the various entries, are Charley Schaefer of the Detroit Tigers and Cy Seymour of the New York Giants. At Hot Springs in the spring of 1907 the Detroit team was doing its preliminary training, and as there was a race-meeting at Chittington Park, it is needless to add that the track received its share of patronage from the members of the Tigers. Schaefer once had an extremely lucky day in picking the winners, while I had the worst kind of luck, my selections not being in the running at all. While not a heavy bettor I was very sore over my poor luck, and Schaefer, who was cashing bet after bet, sympathized with me. He said, "Never mind, Ash, you will have better luck next time. In fact, I got a hot one for tomorrow." "What is it? Give it to me now," I said, being scarcely able to conceal my anxiety. "No, wait until tomorrow," continued Schaefer; "be at the hotel in the morning and I will let you have it then, not now." Bright and early I was at the hotel. Encountering Schaefer, I reminded him of his promise of the previous day to hand me a hot one. Grasping me by the arm he led me to a secluded spot and exacted from me a promise not to let anybody else in on this good thing. Then in a stage whisper he gave me the tip, "Shish, Ash, not a word. It's Lunch, 12 to 2."

Cy's Tip.

IN 1907 the racing game had an enormous hold on the players, especially one club, a member of the National League. That season I was in charge of the St. Paul club of the American Association. I had the misfortune to have Roy Hartzell, a member of the St. Louis club, who was loaned to me, recalled in midseason. This of course put me in a bad hole, as it broke up my entire infield. I burned up the wires in my desperation trying to land a man to fill the gap left by Hartzell's recall, and among those I wired was my old friend Cy Seymour. I wired as follows:

"Cy Seymour, care of New York Baseball Club, New York, N. Y.

"Am badly crippled. See McGraw and ask him to let me have infielder Hannifan.
    "Signed: Ed. Ashenback."

The reply came in due time and read as follows:
"Ed. Ashenback, Manager St. Paul B. B. C., St. Paul, Minn. McGraw unable to secure waivers on Hannifan. Place a swell bet on Lady Esther.
    "Signed: Cy Seymour."

Observations in the Dining Room.

IT is always interesting to observe the debut of a young player in the dining room. He is keenly watched by his older teammates and if the youngster eats mostly with his knife, he is instantly dubbed the "sword-swallower." Many are the tales told on the youngsters, and it's on the spring trips that he usually falls a victim to the chaffing of his teammates. On a southern trip, one of these bushers* was seated at a dining table, when one of his teammates asked the waiter for a napkin. "Busher" startled everybody at the table by asking the waiter to bring "him

---
*Busher, a young fellow just starting out, and a term applied to the youngster by the older players.

HUGHEY JENNINGS
Manager of the Detroit Tigers

a plate of them, too." Another busher startled a couple of fellow-players, by asking what in blazes cantaloupe was. "Why, muskmelon or sugarmelon," they explained to him. While they were all laughing at his ignorance, busher Number Two convulsed everybody by saying laughingly, "Ho, ho, ha, ha, the dag-gone fool believes it."

However, it is not always the bushers who are guilty in these dining-room episodes. Old Eagle Eye Jake Beckley, long and favorably known in the major leagues, while a member of the Cincinnati club, pulled one off on himself at a Philadelphia hotel during the club's visit to the Quaker City. At breakfast one morning the waiter brought Jake a tablet and pencil, on which to write out his order for the morning meal. Beckley took the tablet, and desiring a couple of eggs, he made two marks on the tablet. Jake's eyes nearly bulged out of his head when the waiter brought him in (11) eleven instead of two eggs.

In the early nineties, Gus Schmelz, famed for being the only manager who wore a full set of whiskers, was in the National League. Gus had on his team that year none other than the late Bad Bill Eagan. On a trip to Pittsburg the club stopped at a swell hostelry and Bill figured in a couple of laughable incidents. In the dining-room one day, Eagan was handed a tablet and pencil to give the expectant waiter his order. Bill, however, was a very poor scholar, and was loud in his denunciations of a hotel that asked its guests to give written orders for their meals. At this same hotel, Eagan dropped into the dining-room one morning. Bill had put in a joyful night and was just turning in when he passed the dining-room and beheld his manager enjoying an early breakfast. Wanting to make an impression on his manager for being out of bed at so early an hour Bill wandered into the dining-room. As luck would have it, the head waiter seated him at the same table and directly opposite his manager. Now rumor has it that Mr. Schmelz's glorious whiskers played an important part in giving the signals in the games. As soon as Eagan was seated, Schmelz gazed at him, carelessly stroking his whiskers when bing! Eagan shot head-first under the table. Instantly there was a commotion. When the waiters had seized him and hustled him out of the dining-room, Bill gazed remorsefully back at the manager, and said, "What are you fellows putting me out for? Didn't Schmelz give me the sign to slide?"

In 1904 and 1905 I owned the Charleston, S. C., club of the South Atlantic League and had on my club as a first baseman the well-known veteran, Sam LaRocque, and a hustling, fighting, little Irishman from Cincinnati named McKernan. The hotels on the circuit that year were notoriously bad. This was especially hard on LaRocque, who was an immense feeder. We were playing in Macon, Ga., one day and LaRocque was loud in his protest about the hotel. "How can we win any pennants on such food?" he roared. Finally I went out and dug up another hostelry. This hotel was really a good one, so I lost no time in making the change. I was naturally much pleased at my good fortune in landing accommodations in so fine a house. Hunting up LaRocque I took him in charge and showed him through the rooms. "What do you think of this, Sam?" I asked. "A Class C club stopping at so fine a hotel. Why, look at those bathtubs. They are made of solid tile." "Hum, hum," grunted Sam, "who in h—l ever heard of anybody eating bathtubs?"

Nick Altrock, for years one of the Chicago American League club's star pitchers, caused quite a laugh among the guests at the hotel at which his club was stopping. The enterprising landlord had his name and that of his hotel inscribed on every toothpick. Altrock, spying the landlord among a lot of his guests, said in a patronizing sort of way, "Here, shake hands, Mr. Landlord. I want to hand it to you. There is nothing slow about you when it comes to advertising." "Why do you say that," sputtered the bewildered landlord, evidently not understanding Altrock. "Here," said Altrock, "I am wise to you all right," handing him one of his toothpicks. "You want to have your name in everybody's mouth."

One fine Sunday my club was playing at Jacksonville, Fla. The crowd was an immense one and I was in the best of spirits. I was short a man that day so I moved LaRocque over to shortstop and played first base myself. I was cutting up quite a bit around first base, and when we got back to the bench my second baseman, McKernan, was fairly foaming at the mouth. "What do you think of that big Dutchman? Here we are fighting like blazes to win the pennant and him joshing around first base." "Fighting for the pennant?" roared out LaRocque. "Why, you blankety blank fool. All we're fighting for is something to eat."

A Hold-up.

I HAVE been telling so many stories about my friends in this volume that one on myself may not be amiss. Elsewhere in this volume it is told where I owned the Hampton, Va., franchise in the Virginia League, and also how few and far between salary days were for the players.

The poor athletes chased me all over town for their salaries. I kept putting them off from time to time, hoping against hope that the worm would turn at last and the boys would receive at least part of their pay. On my club that season I had an irrepressible red-headed chap named Reddy Gilligan. One morning at the hotel I packed my baggage preparatory to leaving the hotel for cheaper accommodations, for matters were getting worse and worse. Gilligan was on hand bidding me good-morning, when he beheld me packing my trunk. He did not continue his usual morning call, but bowed himself out of my room. He returned in a short time, however, accompanied by five or six players of the team, who entered the room in a most stealthy manner. They guarded the windows and Red was at the door, which he locked. Gilligan said, "Look here, Ash, you've got to settle with me and the gang," pulling out a revolver that looked to be as large as a cannon to me. "We know you're going to duck out of here. Didn't I see you pack your trunk a little while ago?" With this he kept advancing toward me with that awful cannon. "Don't shoot!" I remember yelling. I don't know how I ever told Red and the boys that they were entirely welcome to whatever money I

WILLIAM HART
Who has been pitching good ball for twenty-seven years.

had, and that the League would see that not one penny of their salaries would they lose. My spluttering explanation seemed to satisfy the boys, for they unlocked the door and withdrew. Gilligan, however, remained and again pulling out that cannon said, "I trust you ain't sore, Ash. Myself and the boys believe that you are doing the best you can by us—but here," shoving the cannon under my nose. I took a look at the revolver—and would you believe the thing was an old relic from the Revolutionary War that they had dug up somewhere, in one of the relic stores abounding in Hampton. Gilligan and the boys gave me the scare of my life with it. Later, when fortune smiled upon us once again and we had a pay day, I took the extra precaution to pay off Gilligan first. At this late day whenever I meet a player who heard of the hold-up, I am always greeted with the following, "Hello, Ash. Don't shoot! Don't shoot!"

John McGraw.

THIS gentleman was once known as "Muggsy," but that appellation was dropped at his own request when he won the world's championship for New York in the fall of 1905, in the first world's series which was ever conducted under the auspices of the National Commission. Since that time, the peppery leader of the Giants has been variously known as John, Mac, or Mr. McGraw, depending upon the degree of intimacy which his interlocutor can claim. This noted character was an infielder of great skill for several years, playing third base for the champion Orioles when the Baltimore team was showing the way to all other aggregations. McGraw learned his baseball in the school of Ned Hanlon and Joe Kelley. He has never forgotten what those geniuses taught him and he has added to his knowledge from observation and experience.

McGraw took hold of the New York club when it was a hopeless tail-ender, back in 1903. His master hand produced results at once. The next year he finished second in the National League race and for the next two seasons he landed the pennant, adding to that honor a wonderful victory in the world's series with the Philadelphia Athletics in 1905, when the champions of the American League could win but one out of five games from the Giants, and did not score a run off McGraw's two great pitchers, Mathewson and McGinnity, in any one of the four games which New York won. Since then, McGraw has always had his team well up in the race and fighting for the highest honors. In 1908 he lost the pennant by the narrow margin of one game, through an unusual play in an important game, which was taken from the Giants through the failure of one of the Giant players to touch a base when they had the game practically won.

McGraw is noted for the fighting spirit which he instils into his men. The New Yorks are one of the greatest attractions on the road from a box-office standpoint because the fans know that they are sure to see a scrappy, hard-fought battle when McGraw's team is in town.

It is this quality that has enabled McGraw to keep his team high in the standing year after year, when, on the winter form, the club did not look capable of finishing higher than fourth or fifth.

McGraw was once notorious as a kicker on the field and his troubles with the umpires were of daily occurrence. But he has calmed down of later seasons and is now a model of propriety, though always wide awake to the interests of his club and fearless in demanding all that is coming to him.

McGraw's work with the New York club has been so remarkable that he recently signed a three-year contract at a salary of $18,000 a year, the largest sum received by any manager in the country. And he is worth every cent of this liberal stipend.

Connie Mack.

WHO has not heard of this quiet yet energetic leader of the world's champion Athletics of Philadelphia, in the American League? His defeat of the Cubs was not so much of a surprise to tens of thousands of fans throughout the country. Connie Mack needs no brass band accompaniments to herald his prowess through the country. His record is known to all, so I want to dwell on some of his methods in building up world's champions.

When other clubs in the major leagues were harboring the old-time stars, Mr. Mack was the first manager to go after the youngsters, and while his rival teams were paying thousands and thousands of dollars for talent, the quiet, foxy Celt was at his work and secured bright, hustling recruits who were getting paid for what they were doing and not for what they HAD done. Mack's method was to have a club that was coming, all the time, and you will never hear of any club that he is at the head of falling by the wayside on account of old age, or because the players have outlived their usefulness. In various minor leagues there are dozens of players who have the Connie Mack string on them. During my two years experience in the Tri-State League, if a player looked promising and you wanted to secure him from his club, the reply would invariably be, "He belongs to Connie Mack."

Mr. Mack has first call on every college player of promise in this land, so it would seem. The instant a player shows any promise in any college, other clubs may as well not try to land the promising one, for in some unaccountable and mysterious manner the reply will be, "He is going with Connie Mack." If there is a more universal favorite with the faculties and priests connected with the various universities, colleges and schools than this same Connie Mack, I want to see him. Wherever the Athletics play, there are always plenty of them on hand to welcome Connie. Does this explain Mack's wonderful success in landing the best talent right out of the cradle? Jack Tighe, the clever manager who won three or four pennants out in the I–I–I–League, is a great admirer of Connie. At a recent meeting of the National Association at Chicago, there was a fan-fest among various managers who were present. Of course Mack's name came up. "By gorroh," said Tighe, "I consider him the best manager in the business. Why, I figure Mack a greater man than Roosevelt, and I will tell you why. When Roosevelt returned from his triumphal hunting trip through Africa he was due for an audience with His Holiness the Pope at Rome. But instead, Teddy got, the can and never did get to see His Holiness. How different with Connie. On his bridal tour he visited Rome, where he not only received an audience with His Holiness, but the eminent Cardinals present engaged him in a fan-fest, asking why he did not pitch Eddie Plank in the world's series, etc. Roosevelt,—Bah!"

Hughey Jennings.

I WANT to tell you a few words about one of the greatest managers in the country today, a fighter in every sense of the word, who from the tap of the bell is on the coaching lines, urging his men on to victory. When a run or two behind you will hear him on the lines, "Come on, boys, it's only a matter of time until we get them." He and the word "quit" are strangers of the most pronounced type. Such a man is Hughey Jennings, who worked his way from the bottom of the baseball ladder into the very zenith of professional balldom. His record of coming into the American League direct from the minors and rounding a poor second-division club into a three-time-pennant-winner, as he did with the Detroit club, is known to every fan throughout the land. He has advanced steadily from the time he left the coal-mines around his home near Scranton, Pa., and donned the mask and protector with a semi-professional club at Lehighton, Pa. It is not of his grand record however, that I want to speak, but of his sterling qualities as a man. In 1905-1906 I was the manager in Jennings' home town—Scranton—and if there was one solitary man in that hustling mining city who had an ill word for Hughey, I failed to meet him. Sharing baseball in Jennings' mind is his great love for his old folks. From the moment he was handed any salary he always took care of his parents and educated his smaller brothers. It was for their comfort that he was hustling all the time. I want to mention a little incident that happened at the close of our baseball season at Scranton in 1905. Jennings was then manager of the Baltimore club and we played an exhibition game at Scranton on the day after the regular season closed. The Baltimore players arrived in due time and, as is usual, were the center of an admiring crowd, because they were "Our-Hughey's" team. The crowd tried to take charge of Hughey, evidently intending to dine and entertain him before the game. But there was no entertainment just then—there may have been after the game—for Jennings' thoughts were elsewhere. On the hill at a Sisters' Convent was one—his little motherless daughter, who was by far dearer than all the baseball-loving fans in the world. Is it any wonder that a man of that caliber is successful?

Before They Were Big Leaguers.

AUGUST HERRMANN, Chairman National Commission, was a city official in Cincinnati; Ban B. Johnson, President American League, was a newspaper writer in Cincinnati; Thos. J. Lynch, President National League, umpire and theater-owner; Connie Mack, millhand in Massachusetts; Frank L. Chance, rancher in California; Hal. Chase, student, Santa Clara College, California; John J. McGraw, shop hand at Truxton, N. Y.; Hugh Jennings, miner at Avoca, Penn.; Fred Clarke, farmer in Kansas; Pat Donovan, druggist at Lawrence, Mass.; Chas. Dooin, clothing-cutter at Cincinnati; Napoleon Lajoie, cab-driver at Woonsocket, R. I.; Clark Griffith, rancher in Montana; James McAleer, haberdasher at Youngstown, Ohio; Roger Bresnahan, detective at Toledo, Ohio; Fred Lake, millhand at Lowell, Mass.

Don'ts For Young Players.

DON'T—imagine you are going to a picnic when entering the profession. It's only hard, conscientious work that leads to success.

DON'T—hesitate to ask your manager if in doubt on any play or subject. He is there for that purpose and will be glad to enlighten you.

DON'T—think that when your manager, captain or one of your older teammates calls your attention to any weakness you may display that they are abusing you. They have only your interests at heart, and are ever ready to assist you.

DON'T—in event you make an error of omission or commission, make an excuse and shift the blame on a fellow-player. Take your medicine. You are not deceiving your manager, and remember it's but human to err.

DON'T—when fortune smiles upon you in your work, let your head get swelled and imagine the club cannot do without your services. Don't forget the old southern adage, "A hoss that runs fast, may not run long."

DON'T—when you are up against a streak of misfortune, whine and hang your head. There is an old saying, "After rain comes sunshine."

DON'T—when off the playing field, let everybody in town know that you are a ballplayer. Conduct yourself as a gentleman at all times. Players of the present day need no brass band accompaniments to let the public know that they are athletes.

DON'T—when playing, take your mind off your work by jawing at the umpire. It distracts your thinking apparatus, when your attention should be on the game.

DON'T—be a crab when one of your fellow-players makes an error, or your pitcher is a bit wild. Pat him on the back with a "Never mind, old man, you will do better next time." We all have our share of bad days.

WILLIAM J. CLYMER
One of the Greatest of Managers

DON'T—constantly growl at your fellow-players. Fault-finders and growlers are not tolerated by managers. You can always catch more flies with sugar than you can with vinegar.

DON'T—eat with your knife. The day of the sword-swallower is past.

DON'T—when you meet with a slight accident, such as stumbling over a blade of grass, or getting a mosquito-bite, loaf, and stay out of the game. In olden days players played with broken limbs for fear of being replaced.

DON'T—threaten to shoot, stab or murder any baseball scribe when some adverse criticism falls to your lot. Remember the scribe is there for that purpose, and where you are handed one knock, a dozen bouquets come your way. And above all things remember that "A little drop of ink has made nations think."

DON'T—constantly nag the umpire. It will get you NOTHING. The late Mike Kelly once said, "After all the kicking I did with those fellows in the past ten years, I at this time fail to see where they gave me anything worse than an even break."

DON'T—mind anybody's business but your own. Never carry tales. "A silent man's words are not brought into court."

DON'T—forget that you cannot think of two things at once. Keep your mind on the game.

DON'T—when your manager tells you to go up to the plate and sacrifice, growl because you are not told to hit it out. Remember, your manager is playing for runs and not hits. The former win games, not the latter.

DON'T—whine and growl at poor hotel accommodations. Have you as good accommodations at home?

DON'T—loaf when the season is drawing to a close and you are longing for home. Remember, your last two weeks' salary is the same as the first two weeks. Besides, your manager may hand you a contract the next spring calling for a shorter season.

DON'T—make yourself a petty larceny or doormat thief, by carrying home the club's uniforms and sweaters at the close of the season. Ofttimes they may be had for the asking.

Don'ts for the Baseball Fans.

DON'T—slap a man in front of you on the back every time a home player does something that calls for commendation. He may be betting the other way—and be handy with his fists.

DON'T—imagine for a moment that the batsman is going to knock the cover off the ball just because you have admonished him to do so. He would try just as hard if you were not within a mile of the ballground.

DON'T—swear at the shortstop if the grounder he expects to catch about knee-high takes a sudden bound and hits him in the nose. Tacks and other obstacles have been known to intrude themselves even on a ballroom floor.

HUMOR AMONG THE MINORS

DON'T—call the batter a dub because he fails to put out a home run when the bases are full. If he goes out on an easy play, try to think that, in the baseball profession, the pitchers are paid just a trifle more for preventing home runs at such a stage of the game than the batter for making them.

DON'T—make an exhibition of yourself by calling loudly to have the umpire killed if he makes a decision that looks as if it favored the opposing team. Remember, he is nearer the play than you are, and that you would not lay a hand on him if you had the opportunity.

DON'T—allow the idea to get possession of your mind that, unless you yell so that nothing else can be heard on the grounds, the home team will lose. Rational rooting and encouragement are the proper things at a game. Lung-splitting is to be discouraged for physical and mental reasons.

DON'T—let the people around you know that you are wise on everything pertaining to baseball. There may be an old ballplayer or a newspaper man in the vicinity who will challenge your statements and incidentally reduce your appearance to something akin to a plugged quarter or a pewter five-cent piece.

Managing a Baseball Team.

BY AN OLD-TIME AND SUCCESSFUL EX-NATIONAL LEAGUE MANAGER.

KNOW your men intimately.

Handle each man as his disposition requires.

Appeal to the player's intelligence, giving reasons for your instructions.

Play no favorites, thus giving no man cause for being discontented.

Ask no man to do that which you would shrink from doing yourself.

Be sufficiently intimate with your players to have a grip on them; sufficiently distant to cause no jealousy.

Have as few rules as possible, but see to it that all rules laid down are implicitly obeyed.

Instill into your players a sufficient amount of fighting spirit to make them feel that there always is a chance to win.

Get into no arguments or controversies of any kind with your players.

You are in command and your word must be law.

Make your players feel that they are at liberty at all times to make suggestions, which will be received with careful consideration.

Make your own observations regarding the conduct of your players. Pay no attention to the many rumors that always crop out regarding players.

CHARLEY SCHAEFER
A Clever Minor League Manager

Convince your men right at the start that you mean business; that they must attend to business, and their business is to play baseball to the best of their ability until after the last game has been decided.

N. B.—After adhering strictly to the above laid-down rules: Sign Jack Johnson as official trainer—to keep the rough necks off you. Purchase at least one Colt's 45-calibre revolver, and the path at the head of the Never-Win Clippers will be strewn with nothing but roses, and pennants will come in bunches.

To A Young Leaguer.

"Do Not Give Up."

With Apologies to Byron Woodward Goodsell.

When anything you try goes bad,
Heads up, don't feel sad.
When the fans seem cold to you,
And your life looks drear and blue,
        Do Not Give Up.

When at the bat they won't go safe,
Don't whine, complain and chafe.
Do not worry or despair,
Base-hits will yet come free as air,
        Do Not Give Up.

When you happen to make a boot
And hear the cruel knocker's hoot,
If you know you are in the right,
Hold your ground and make the fight,
        Do Not Give Up.

Time and tide may seem to say
You have missed the easy way;
Even if your path be dark and lone,
Have faith that you will land at home,
        Do Not Give Up.

MILEAGE TABLES

THE NATIONAL LEAGUE

TO FROM	NEW YORK	PHILA-DELP'A	BOSTON	BROOK-LYN	ST. LOUIS	PITTS-BURG	CHI-CAGO	CINCIN-NATI
New York....	Correct	90	231	1	976	445	913	758
Philadelphia..	90	Mileage	321	91	886	354	823	668
Boston	231	321	Of	232	1226	765	1033	925
Brooklyn	1	91	231	Nat'l	887	446	914	758
St. Louis....	976	886	1226	887	League	623	283	339
Pittsburg ...	445	354	765	446	623	Base	468	313
Chicago......	913	823	1033	914	283	468	Ball	298
Cincinnati...	758	668	925	759	339	313	298	Clubs

The American League

TO \ FROM	NEW YORK	PHILA-DELP'A	WASH-INGTON	BOS-TON	ST. LOUIS	CHI-CAGO	DE-TROIT	CLEVE-LAND
New York ...	Correct	90	227	231	976	913	809	621
Philadelphia..	90	Mileage	137	321	886	823	864	682
Washington ..	227	137	Of	457	939	913	681	621
Boston	231	321	457	Ameri'n	1226	1033	749	855
St. Louis	976	886	939	1226	League	283	567	548
Chicago......	913	823	913	1033	283	Base	284	357
Detroit	809	864	681	649	567	284	Ball	178
Cleveland	621	682	621	855	548	357	178	Clubs

The American Association

TO FROM	COLUM- BUS	INDIAN- APOLIS	KANSAS CITY	LOUIS- VILLE	MIL- WA'KE	MINNE- APOLIS	ST. PAUL	TOLE- DO
Columbus....	Correct	188	802	230	399	756	745	123
Indianapolis..	188	Mileage	466	110	280	615	605	24
Kansas City..	802	466	Of	671	574	597	587	702
Louisville	230	110	671	Ameri'n	390	810	800	325
Milwaukee ...	399	280	574	390	Assoc'n	335	325	329
Minneapolis ..	756	615	597	810	335	Base	10	664
St. Paul......	745	605	587	800	325	10	Ball	664
Toledo	123	240	702	325	329	664	654	Clubs

The Eastern League

TO FROM	BUF-FALO	ROCH-'TER	JERSEY CITY	TORON-TO	MON-TREAL	NEW-ARK	PROVI-DENCE	BALTI-MORE
Buffalo......	Correct	68	408	101	439	402	641	396
Rochester....	68	Mileage	340	169	507	332	573	464
Jersey City...	408	340	Of	509	451	6	188	185
Toronto......	101	169	509	Eastern	333	515	697	497
Montreal.....	439	507	451	333	League	458	374	636
Newark......	402	346	6	515	458	Base	194	179
Providence...	641	573	188	697	382	194	Ball	374
Baltimore....	396	464	185	497	636	179	374	Clubs

The Southern League

TO \ FROM	NEW ORL'S	ATLAN-TA	MEM-PHIS	NASH-VILLE	MONT-GOM'Y	CHAT-TAN'GA	BIRM-INGH'M	MOBILE
New Orleans..	Correct	496	396	624	321	492	349	141
Atlanta.......	496	Mileage	419	289	175	138	168	355
Memphis.....	396	419	South'n	333	347	310	251	527
Nashville.....	624	289	333	League	303	162	207	483
Montgomery .	321	175	347	303	Base	313	96	180
Chattanooga..	492	138	310	162	313	Ball	143	419
Birmingham...	349	168	251	207	96	143	Clubs	276
Mobile.......	141	355	527	483	180	419	276	Class A

The Western League

TO FROM	SIOUX CITY	DEN-VER	LIN-COLN	WICH-ITA	OMAHA	ST. JO-SEPH	DES MOINES	TOPEKA
Sioux City.....	Correct	565	82	240	27	156	142	85
Denver........	567	Mileage	593	581	538	644	653	573
Lincoln........	82	593	Weste'n	424	55	184	170	269
Wichita........	240	581	424	League	369	226	370	155
Omaha........	27	538	55	369	Base	129	115	214
St. Joseph.....	156	644	184	226	129	Ball	144	71
Des Moines...	142	653	170	370	115	144	Class A	215
Topeka........	85	573	269	155	214	71	215	League

The Central League

TO FROM	DAYTON	EVANS-VILLE	CANTON	GRAND RAPIDS	SPRING-FIELD	SOUTH BEND	TERRE HAUTE	WHEEL-ING
Dayton......	Correct	279	232	276	35	214	283	204
Evansville....	279	Mileage	501	488	314	385	110	557
Canton.......	232	501	Of	362	207	193	391	167
Grand Rapids.	276	488	362	Central	311	275	275	529
Springfield....	35	314	207	311	League	249	318	179
South Bend...	214	385	193	275	249	Base	182	360
Terre Haute..	283	110	391	275	318	182	Ball	520
Wheeling.....	204	557	167	529	179	360	520	Clubs

The I-I-I League

TO FROM	SPRING- FIELD	ROCK ISLAND	PEORIA	WATER- LOO	BLOOM- INGTON	DU- BUQUE	DAVEN- PORT	DAN- VILLE
Springfield....	Correct	154	63	335	59	236	157	128
Rock Island...	154	Mileage	91	179	136	104	3	217
Peoria.........	63	91	I-I-I	294	45	195	94	126
Waterloo......	335	179	294	League	187	99	180	420
Bloomington..	59	136	45	187		240	139	81
Dubuque......	236	104	195	99	240		101	321
Davenport....	157	3	94	180	139	101		127
Danville.......	128	217	126	420	81	321	127	

The Pacific Coast League

FROM \ TO	SAN FRAN'O	PORT-LAND	LOS ANGEL'S	SACRA-MENTO	OAK-LAND	VERNON
San Francisco	Correct	772	482	90	4	482
Portland	772	Mileage	1254	682	768	1254
Los Angeles	482	1254	Of	572	568	2
Sacramento	90	682	572	Pacific	86	572
Oakland	4	768	568	86	Coast	482
Vernon	482	1254	2	572	482	League

The New York State League

TO \ FROM	SYRA-CUSE	TROY	ALBANY	UTICA	WILKES-BARRE	SCRAN-TON	ELMIRA	BING-HAMT'N
Syracuse......	Correct	152	147	63	160	142	127	80
Troy.........	152	Mileage	5	99	233	215	205	148
Albany.......	147	5	New	94	218	210	200	143
Utica	63	99	94	York	175	157	139	82
Wilkesbarre ..	160	233	228	175	State	18	137	80
Scrantorr.....	142	215	210	157	18	League	119	62
Elmira........	127	205	200	139	137	119		57
Binghamton..	80	148	143	82	80	62	57	

The New England League

TO FROM	WOR-CES'R	BROCK-TON	LYNN	FALL RIVER	HAVER-HILL	NEW BEDF'D	LOW-ELL	LAW-RENCE
Worcester	Correct	53	65	93	88	89	79	83
Brockton	53	Mileage	32	83	53	76	51	59
Lynn	65	32	New	61	45	68	38	51
Fall River	93	83	61	Engl'nd	86	7	75	79
Haverhill	88	53	45	86	League	89	5	6
New Bedford	89	76	68	7	89		88	86
Lowell	79	51	38	75	5	88		13
Lawrence	83	59	51	79	6	86	13	

The Connecticut League

TO FROM	HART- FORD	SPRING- FIELD	WATER- BURY	NEW HAVEN	NEW BRIT'N	NORTH- HAM'N	BRIDGE- PORT	HOL- YOKE
Hartford.....	Correct	31	32	36	8	48	54	39
Springfield.....	31	Mileage	63	62	34	17	80	8
Waterbury.....	32	63	Conn.	25	23	80	32	71
New Haven...	36	74	25	League	28	76	18	44
New Britain...	39	34	23	28		51	46	42
Northampton.	48	17	80	76	51		94	9
Bridgeport....	54	80	69	18	46	94		88
Holyoke......	39	8	71	44	42	25	88	

The Tri-State League

TO FROM	HARRIS- BURG	YORK	TREN- TON	ALTOO- NA	READ- ING	LAN- CASTER	JOHNS- TOWN	WIL- M'NGT'N
Harrisburg...	Correct	28	139	131	54	37	169	132
York.........	28	Mileage	167	159	82	65	197	131
Trenton......	139	167	Tri-	270	90	102	309	51
Altoona......	131	159	270	State	185	168	38	262
Reading......	54	82	90	185	League	42	223	83
Lancaster....	37	65	102	168	42		206	94
Johnstown...	169	197	309	38	223	206		300
Wilmington..	132	131	51	262	83	94	300	

The Northwestern League

FROM \ TO	SPOKANE	SEATTLE	TACOMA	VICTORIA	PORT-LAND	VAN-COUVER
Spokane........	Correct	40	386	150	540	218
Seattle........	40	Mileage	21	110	140	178
Tacoma........	386	21	Of	150	144	131
Victoria........	150	110	150	The	195	84
Portland...•••	540	140	144	195	North-western	279
Vancouver......	218	178	131	84	279	League

The Western Association

TO FROM	SPRING-FIELD	MUSKO-GEE	EL RENO	SAPULPA	GUTHRIE	ENID
Springfield, Mo.	Correct	219	331	210	294	307
Muskogee, I.T.	219	Mileage	264	71	278	325
El Reno	331	264	Of	349	41	61
Sapulpa	210	71	349	The	94	107
Guthrie, Okla.	294	278	41	94	Western	56
Enid, Okla.	307	325	61	107	56	Associat'n

The Ohio and Pennsylvania League

TO FROM	YOUNGSTOWN	MANSFIELD	AKRON	CANTON	ERIE	M'KEESPORT	NEW CASTLE	E. LIVERPOOL
Youngstown...	Correct	252	55	77	79	92	19	120
Mansfield....	252	Mileage	96	74	230	190	233	218
Akron........	55	96	Of	20	134	147	74	175
Canton	77	74	20	The	156	116	159	144
Erie.........	79	230	134	156	Ohio	162	185	167
McKeesport..	92	190	147	116	162	and	78	58
New Castle...	19	233	74	159	182	78	Penna.	101
East Liverpool	120	218	175	144	167	58	101	League

The Virginia League

TO FROM	NORFOLK	LYNCH-BURG	RICH-MOND	DAN-VILLE	ROANOKE	PORTS-MOUTH
Norfolk......	Mileage	204	85	270	257	1
Lynchburg....	204	Of	146	66	53	205
Richmond.....	85	146	Virginia	141	199	86
Danville.....	270	66	141	League	119	271
Roanoke......	257	53	199	119	Class	258
Portsmouth...	1	205	86	271	258	(C)

The South Atlantic League

TO FROM	AUGUS-TA	CHARL'S-TON	COLUM-BIA	JACKS'N-VILLE	MACON	SAVAN-NAH	ALBA-NY	COLUM-BUS
Augusta........	Mileage	138	82	304	125	132	232	225
Charleston....	138	Of	129	287	263	115	370	363
Columbia......	82	129	South Atlantic	314	207	142	314	314
Jacksonville..	304	287	314	League	262	172	187	287
Macon.........	125	263	207	262	Of	172	107	100
Savannah......	132	115	142	172	172	Base-ball	279	272
Albany........	232	370	314	187	107	279	Clubs	100
Columbus	225	363	314	287	100	272	100	Class C

The Western Canada League

TO FROM	BRANDON	CALGARY	EDMONTON	LETHBRIDGE	MEDI'N HAT	MOOSE JAW	REGINA	WINNIPEG
Brandon......	Correct	707	899	765	658	266	225	133
Calgary.......	707	Mileage	192	287	180	441	482	840
Edmonton.....	899	192	Of	479	372	533	674	1032
Lethbridge....	765	287	479	The	107	368	293	287
Medicine Hat.	658	180	372	107	West'n	261	41	399
Moose Jaw....	266	441	533	368	261	Canada	41	399
Regina.......	225	482	674	293	186	41	League	358
Winnipeg.....	133	840	1032	287	180	399	358	

The Wisconsin-Illinois League

TO FROM	ROCK- FORD	APPLE- TON	FOND DU LAC	OSH- KOSH	RACINE	MAD- ISON	AURO- RA	GREEN BAY
Rockford......	Correct	204	169	186	82	82	137	230
Appleton......	204	Mileage	35	17	124	124	231	26
Fond du Lac..	169	35	Wis.	35	87	89	194	65
Oshkosh......	186	17	35	Illinois	104	124	211	48
Racine........	82	124	87	104	League	129	107	152
Madison......	82	124	89	124	129		219	150
Aurora........	137	231	194	211	107	219		257
Green Bay....	230	26	65	48	152	150	257	

The Nebraska State League

TO FROM	HAST-INGS	RED CLOUD	COLUM-BUS	SUPE-RIOR	SEWARD	KEAR-NEY	FRE-MONT	GRAND ISLAND
Hastings....	Correct	41	61	51	75	37	126	25
Red Cloud...	41	Mileage	102	24	116	78	167	66
Columbus....	61	102	Of	70	46	105	35	36
Superior.....	51	24	70	The	83	88	146	76
Seward......	75	116	46	83	Neb.	112	63	67
Kearney.....	37	78	105	88	112	State	150	63
Fremont.....	126	167	35	146	63	150	League	107
Grand Island..	25	66	36	76	67	63	107	

The Southwestern Texas League

TO FROM	CORPUS CHRISTI	BROWNS-VILLE	BAY CITY	BEE-VILLE	LAREDO	VICTORIA
Corpus Christi...	Correct	158	139	56	160	110
Brownsville......	158	Mileage	297	214	318	268
Bay City........	139	297	Of	84	216	29
Beeville........	56	214	84	South-western	216	55
Laredo..........	160	318	216	216	Texas	271
Victoria........	111	268	29	55	271	League

—201

The Eastern Kansas League

FROM \ TO	SENECA	HOLTON	HIAWATHA	HORTON	SABETHA	MARYSVILLE
Seneca.......	Correct	36	34	40	16	36
Holton.......	36	Mileage	42	20	48	72
Hiawatha.....	34	42	Of	22	18	74
Horton.......	40	20	22	Eastern	24	94
Sabetha......	16	48	18	24	Kansas	52
Marysville...	36	72	74	94	52	League

The Northern State League of Indiana

FROM \ TO	MARION	BLUFFTON	KOKOMO	LAFAYETTE	WABASH	HUNTINGTON
Marion.........	Correct	30	27	75	20	39
Bluffton........	30	Mileage	51	107	50	49
Kokomo.........	27	57	Of	50	47	66
Lafayette.......	75	107	50	Northern State League	66	85
Wabash.........	20	50	47	66	Of	19
Huntington.....	39	49	66	85	19	Indiana

The Southeastern League

TO FROM	ASHE-VILLE	JOHNSON CITY	MORRIS-TOWN	KNOX-VILLE	ROME	GADSDEN
Asheville......	Correct	163	87	129	318	238
Johnson City	163	Mileage	76	118	309	227
Morristown......	87	76	Of	42	233	120
Knoxville.......	129	118	42	The	191	109
Rome...........	318	309	233	191	South-eastern	300
Gadsden	238	227	120	109	300	League

The West-Virginia League

FROM \ TO	MANNINGTON	CLARKSBURG	GRAFTON	FAIRMOUNT
Mannington......	Correct	62	40	18
Clarksburg......	62	Mileage	22	33
Grafton......	40	22	West-Virginia	55
Fairmount......	18	33	55	League

HUMOR AMONG THE MINORS

THE SAN JOAQUIN VALLEY LEAGUE

FROM \ TO	BAKERSFIELD	VISALIA	COALINGS	TULARE
Bakersfield, Cal.....	Correct	66	105	63
Visalia, Cal.....	66	Mileaeg	39	10
Coalings, Cal.....	105	39	San Joaquin Valley	49
Tulare, Cal.....	63	10	49	League

The Indiana-Michigan League

TO FROM	ELKHART	GARY	GOSHEN	NILES	BERRIEN SPRINGS	BENTON HARBOR
Elkhart........	Correct	120	11	20	29	44
Gary..........	120	Mileage	130	140	149	164
Goshen........	11	130	Of	30	39	54
Niles..........	20	140	30	Indiana	9	58
Berrien Springs..	29	149	39	9	Michigan	15
Benton Harbor...	44	164	54	58	15	League

The Texas Association

TO FROM	DENNI-SON	PARIS	SHER-MAN	CORSI-CANA	PALES-TINE	TAYLOR	CLE-BURNE
Dennison......	Correct	69	9	218	214	268	161
Paris..........	69	Mileage	60	150	108	173	151
Sherman.......	9	60	Of	227	203	257	152
Corsicana.....	218	150	227	The	131	129	105
Palestine......	214	108	203	131	Texas	145	236
Taylor.........	268	173	257	129	145	Asso'n.	113
Cleburne......	161	151	152	105	236	113	

The Carolina Association

TO FROM	GREEN-VILLE	CHAR-LOTTE	WINSTON-SALEM	SPARTAN-BURG	ANDER-SON	GREENS-BORO
Greenville......	Correct	107	229	29	124	200
Charlotte.......	107	Mileage	83	78	227	93
Winston-Salem .	229	83	Carolina	161	310	29
Spartanburg....	29	78	161	Assoc'n	149	171
Anderson.......	124	227	310	149		320
Greensboro.....	200	93	29	171	320	

The Eastern Carolina League

FROM \ TO	GOLDS-BORO	FAYETTE-VILLE	RALEIGH	ROCKY MOUNT	WILSON	WILMING-TON
Goldsboro.......	Correct	50	49	40	24	84
Fayetteville.....	50	Mileage	76	90	74	34
Raleigh.........	49	76	Of	70	54	110
Rocky Mount....	40	90	70	Eastern	16	124
Wilson	24	74	54	16	Carolina	108
Wilmington......	84	34	110	124	108	League

The Cotton States League

FROM \ TO	VICKSBURG	JACKSON	YAZOO CITY	HATTIES-BURG	GREEN-WOOD
Vicksburg	Correct	40	85	225	138
Jackson	40	Mileage	45	181	98
Yazoo City	85	45	Cotton	279	53
Hattiesburg	225	181	279	States	183
Greenwood	138	98	53	183	League

The Kentucky-Illinois-Tennessee League

TO FROM	VIN-CENNES	PADUCAH	HENDER-SON	MADISON-VILLE	CLARKS-VILLE	HOPKINS-VILLE
Vincennes......	Correct	215	65	103	176	139
Paducah.......	215	Mileage	138	176	111	212
Henderson.....	103	138	Kentucky	38	111	74
Madisonville...	65	176	38	Illinois	73	36
Clarksville.....	176	111	111	73	Tennessee	37
Hopkinsville...	139	212	74	36	37	League

The Virginia Valley League

FROM \ TO	HUNTING-TON	CHARLES-TON	PT. PLEAS-ANT	ASHLAND-CATL'SB'G	PARKERS-BURG	MONT-GOMERY
Huntington......	Correct	50	53	10	121	77
Charleston.......	50	Mileage	99	60	177	27
Pt. Pleasant......	53	99	Of	131	78	136
Ashland-Catlettsburg.	10	60	131	The	131	93
Parkersburg......	121	177	78	131	Virginia Valley	204
Montgomery......	77	27	136	93	204	League

HUMOR AMONG THE MINORS

The Blue Grass League

TO FROM	PARIS	LEXING-TON	RICH-MOND	WIN-CHESTER	FRANK-FORT	MAYS-VILLE
Paris.........	Correct	18	39	18	68	50
Lexington.....	18	Mileage	22	18	49	64
Richmond......	39	22	Of	23	71	89
Winchester....	18	18	23	Blue	48	66
Frankfort.....	68	49	71	48	Grass	118
Maysville.....	50	64	89	66	118	League

The Ohio State League

FROM \ TO	PORTS-MOUTH	MARION	LIMA	LAN-CASTER	NEWARK	CHILLI-COTHE
Portsmouth.....	Correct	145	197	131	133	49
Marion.........	145	Mileage	46	76	78	94
Lima...........	197	46	Of	124	157	140
Lancaster......	131	76	124	The	64	82
Newark.........	133	78	157	64	Ohio State	84
Chillicothe.....	49	94	140	82	84	League

The Central Association

TO FROM	QUINCY	OTTUM-WA	HAN-NIBAL	GALES-BURG	KEO-KUK	MON-MOUTH	BUR-LINGT'N	KEWA-NEE
Quincy......	Correct	137	20	100	41	84	72	132
Ottumwa......	137	Mileage	157	117	76	101	60	149
Hannibal......	20	157	Of	119	61	104	101	151
Galesburg......	100	117	119	Central	86	16	43	32
Keokuk......	41	76	61	86	Assoc'n	70	43	118
Monmouth...	84	101	104	16	70	Base	43	48
Burlington..	72	60	101	43	43	43	Ball	55
Kewanee.....	132	149	151	32	118	48	55	Clubs

The Michigan State League

FROM \ TO	HOLLAND	TRAVERSE CITY	MUSKEGON	CADILLAC
Holland......	Correct	174	23	123
Traverse City....	174	Mileage	183	47
Muskegon......	23	47	Michigan	136
Cadillac......	123	47	136	State League

The South Michigan League

TO \ FROM	KALA-MAZOO	LAN-SING	ADRIAN	BATTLE CREEK	FLINT	JACK-SON	BAY CITY	SAGI-NAW
Kalamazoo....	Correct	94	114	23	117	68	183	179
Lansing.......	94	Mileage	82	71	49	36	79	85
Adrian........	114	82	Of	91	131	46	146	114
Battle Creek..	23	71	91	South	94	45	206	145
Flint.........	117	49	131	94	Mich.	85	45	33
Jackson.......	68	36	46	45	85	League	115	100
Bay City.....	183	79	146	206	45	115		16
Saginaw......	179	85	114	145	33	100	16	

INDEX

Page numbers in *italics* refer to illustrations.
Those ending in (fn) indicate footnotes.

Aberdeen, Washington, 22
Abilene, Kansas, 20
Abilene, Texas, xvi–xvii
Ada, Kansas, 20
Adrian, Michigan, 21, 218
African Americans,
  playing against a white team, 51
Akron, Ohio, 19, 195
Alameda, California, 24
Albany (New York) Senators, xxv
Albany, Georgia, 19, 197
Albany, New York, 18, 51, 72, 189
Alexander, Grover Cleveland, xxx
Allen, W. P., 20
Allentown Colts, xv
Allentown, Pennsylvania, 8, 35
Alloway, Podge, 95
Altizer, Dave, 29, 30
Altoona Mountaineers, xxix
Altoona, Pennsylvania, xvi, 11, 18, 28, 32–34, 91, 97, 124, 156, 192
Altrock, Nick, xviii–xix, xviii(fn), 54, 107, 128–131
American Association, xxvi, 11, 17, 29, 68, 99–101, 117, 127, 148, 159, 182
American Association (major league), 115
American League, 13, 15, 16, 29, 34, 40, 54, 104, 110, 115, 128, 166, 169, 171, 181
Amsterdam, Pennsylvania, 63
Anderson, South Carolina, 22, 209
Anson, Cap, 38, 115
Appleton, Wisconsin, 21, 199
Arkansas City, Kansas, 20

— 219

Armbruster, Charles, 107
Armbruster, Harry, 107
Armour, William, 38
Arndt, Harry, 30
Ashenbach, Edward, 5, 12
   advice on managing, 176, 177
   advice to fans, 174, 175
   advice to young players, 171–174, 178
   alleged abuse of, xxxiv
   and Archibald "Moonlight" Graham, xxi–xxii
   and Christy Mathewson, 40, 132, 133
   and Clark Griffith, xxxiii
   and Cy Seymour, 159, 160
   and Cy Young, 38
   and Eddie Cicotte, 38
   and Harry Coveleski, 103-106
   and Nick Altrock, xx–xxi
   and Ren Mulford, Jr., xiv, xxvi, xxvii, xxvii(fn), xxxiv
   and Ty Cobb, 39
   and origin of the term "bonehead," 73–75
   and the press, 113–115
   as a captain, xx–xxi
   as a club owner, xxi
   as a coach, xix, xxviii, xxix(fn)
   as a manager, 135
   as a scout, xxxii–xxxiii
   as a teammate with players from the South, 49–52
   as Altoona manager, xxv–xxvi, xxix
   as Charleston manager, xix, xxii–xxv
   as Charleston owner, xxii–xxiii, xxiv–xxv
   as Charlotte manager, xxi–xxii
   as college coach, xxi, xxi(fn), 69, 70
   as Evansville manager, xxii
   as Johnstown manager, xxviii, 65–67
   as Nashua manager, xxii
   as Newport News-Hampton manager, xix–xx
   as Scranton manager, xxv–xxvi, xxvii, 51, 63–65, 145, 146, 170
   as St. Paul manager, xxvi–xxvii, 68, 69, 156
   as Syracuse manager, xxix–xxx, xxxii
   as Tarboro manager, xx
   as umpire baiter, 55, 56
   at Abilene, Texas game, xvi–xvii
   begins baseball career, 37
   burial, xxxiv
   catches a pickpocket, 46–48
   considers retirement, xxvii
   death, xxxiv

INDEX

description, xiii, xv–xvi, xxvi
hallucinations, xxiii
humor, xvi, xix, xxvii, xxviii
marriage, xv
mental breakdown, xxxiii–xxxiv
organizes South Atlantic League, 58–60
originates term "bonehead," xxxi–xxxii
potential as a major-leaguer, xvii
reported offer to coach Chicago Cubs, xxviii–xxix
retirement thoughts, xxx
rumors of opportunities to purchase clubs, xxvii–xxviii
spikes a boy, xxiii–xxiv
statistics, xxxii–xxxiii
sued for divorce, xxi
suspended, xxii(fn)
suffers nervous breakdown, xxxii, xxxii(fn)
with Altoona, xvi
with Atlanta, xv–xvi, 49
with Canton, xiv–xv
with Charleston, xx–xxi, 52, 53, 151
with Charlotte, xviii, xix, xx
with Dallas, xvi–xvii, 49, 93, 94
with Evansville, xxii
with Fort Worth, xvi
with Hampton, xviii, 164, 165
with Harrisburg, xv
with Houston, xvii
with Nashua, xx, 53, 54
with New Castle, xvii–xviii
with Newport News, xviii
with Norfolk, xviii
with Paterson, xvii
with Reading, xvi
with Sacramento, xx–xxi
with Schenectady, xviii
with Shenandoah, xvi
with Shreveport, 150–152
with Springfield, xvii, xxxi–xxxii
Ashenbach, Edward H. (son), xxxiv
Ashenbach, Lydia (Westermeir) (wife), xv, xxi, xxxiv
Ashenbach, Mariana (Franke) (mother), xiii
Ashenbach, Joseph (father), xiii
Asheville, North Carolina, 22, 204
Ashland, Kentucky, 23, 213
Atlanta Crackers, xv, xix
Atlanta, Georgia, 8, 18, 19, 49, 93, 108, 109, 111, 184
Atlantic City, New Jersey, 147
Atlantic League, xvii
Aubrey, Harry, xxix
Auburn, New York, 13, 18

HUMOR AMONG THE MINORS

Auburn Falls City, Nebraska, 24
Augusta, Georgia, 19, 38, 39, 58, 60, 68, 96, 97, 197
Aurora, Illinois, 199
Austin, Texas, 20, 123
Avoca, Pennsylvania, 157, 171

Bachman, Lester, 107
Badel, Fred (Humpty), 65–67
Baker, Frank "Home Run," 31
Bakersfield, California, 22, 206
Baldwin, Mark, 35
Baltimore, Maryland, 17, 91, 94, 183
Baltimore Orioles (minor league), 119, 143, 157, 166, 170
Bancroft, Frank, 119
Barger, Eros "Cy," 31
Barney (groundskeeper), 121
Barringer, William H., 23
Barrow, Ed, 17
Bartley, Bill, 107
Barton, Jimmie, 108
Baschang, Al, 108
Bates, Johnny, 32
Battle Creek, Michigan, 21, 218
Baum, Charles, 30, 32
Baxter, xxviii(fn)
Bay City, Wisconsin, 21, 218
Bay City, Texas, 22, 201
Beady, J. H., 131, 132
Beardstown, Illinois, 21
Beaumont, Clarence "Ginger," 117
Beck, Erv, 96, 97
Beckley, Jake, 80, 161
Beeville, Texas, 22, 201
Bell, George, 30, 32
Beloit, Wisconsin, 20
Bender, Charles "Chief," 31
Bennett, 63
Benton Harbor, Michigan, 23, 207
Berrien Springs, Michigan, 23, 207
Bertig, J. R., 21
Binghamton, New York, xxvii, 18, 89, 189
Birmingham, Alabama, 18, 73, 74, 105, 108, 149, 150, 184
Bitman, Red, 107
Blain, A. E., 21
Blair, 31
Bloomington, Indiana, 19, 187
Blough, Ollie, 34
Blue Grass League, xxxii, 20, 96, 214
Bluffton, Indiana, 21, 203
Bockel, Charles, 34
Bockel, Rudy, 32
Boehlein, Bimpy, 109, 110
Bond Hill, Ohio, 118
Bond Hill club, xiv, 6
Bonno, Gus, 108
Boston, Massachusetts, 18, 54, 85, 144, 152
Boston (American League club), 31, 84, 86, 87, 107, 181
Boston (National League club), 30, 101, 180

INDEX

Bowen, J. F., 21
Bowman, Frank, 34
Boyer, Charles, 58
Boyle, Ed, 107
Boyle, Jack, 107
Bradley, W. B., xix
Brand, Buck, 45, 46
Brandon, Manitoba, 19, 198
Bresnahan, Roger, 171
Bridgeport, Connecticut, 18, 86, 88, 191
Bridgeport Unions, 86
Briton, Ollie, 102
Broad Street Station (Philadelphia), 91
Brockton, Massachusetts, 18, 190
Brooklyn (National League club), 30, 32, 54, 107, 108, 116, 180
Brouthers, Art, 50
Brown, Sam, 30
Browning, Pete, 35, 36
Brownsville, Texas, 22, 201
Bruce, John E., *16*, 110
Brush, John T., 9
Bucknell College, 9
Buffalo, New York, 17, 65, 87, 99, 154, 183
Bulger, Bozeman, 73, 74
Burch, Al, 30, 32
Burkett, Jesse, 85
Burlington, Iowa, 21, 216
Burton, California, 23
Bush, Heinie, 108
Bushelman, 108
Button, 71, 72

Cadillac, Michigan, 22, 217

Calgary, Alberta, 19, 198
California Baseball League, 24
California League, xx
Camden, New Jersey, 28
Campbell, Billy, 30
Can Brothers, 119, 120
Can, Lollie-gah-plootz, 119
Can. Snooks, 119
Cantillon, Joe, 29
Canton (Ohio) Deubers, xv
Canton (Ohio) Nadjys, xiv, xiv(fn), xv, xv(fn)
Canton, Illinois, 21
Canton, Ohio, xv, 6, 7, 19, 21, 37, 38, 186, 195
Cargo, Chic, 72
Carlisle Indian Industrial School (Carlisle, Pennsylvania), 145
Carolina Association, 22, 209
Carpenter, Charles F., 18, 28, 34, *112*
Carson, Dr. F. R., 18
Carter, 39
Caruthersville, Missouri, 21
Cassidy, Joe, 31
Catlettsburg, Kentucky, 23, 213
Central Association, 21, 216
Central California Baseball League, 24
Central Kansas League, 20
Central League, xxii, xxvii, 18, 185
Chance, Frank L., xxviii–xxix, 171

—223

Chappelle, 30, 32
Chappelle, Bob, 50, 51
Chard, Jimmie, 109
Charles, 30
Charleston Courier, xxv(fn)
Charleston (South Carolina) Sea Gulls, xix, xxii–xxv, xxv(fn)
Charleston, South Carolina, xx, xxii, 10, 11, 19, 38, 39, 52, 58–60, 63, 151, 197
Charleston, West Virginia, 23, 213
Charlotte Hornets, xxi–xxii
Charlotte, North Carolina, xx, 10, 22, 42-44, *96*, 209
Chase, Hal, 170
Chattanooga Lookouts, xxi
Chattanooga, Tennessee, 18, 43, 62, 92, 115–118, 184
Chehalis, Washington,
Chicago, Illinois, xxxi, 13, 15, 17, 19, 80, 129, 168
Chicago (American League club), 6, 29, 31, 38, 42, 54, 107, 122, 124, 128, 130, 131, 181
Chicago (National League club), 30, 32, 40, 84, 96, 104, 105, 107, 111, 130, 167, 180
   and rumor of hiring Ashenbach to be a coach, xxviii–xxix
Childs, Doc, 50, 51
Childs, Louis, 150–152
Chillicothe, Ohio, 215

Chittington Park (Hot Springs, Arkansas), 158
Chivington, T. M., 17
Cicotte, Eddie, 38, 39
Cincinnati Enquirer, xxx, xxxi
Cincinnati, Ohio, xiii, xv, xvi, xvii, xxxii, xxxiii, xxxiv, 6–9, 37, 66, 67, 92, 106, 107, 110, 111, 115, 118-120, 128–130, 132, 133, 144, 146, 155, 171
   and Seventh Ward Fishing Club, xxvii(fn)
Cincinnati (National League club), xiii, xv, xviii, xxiv, xxviii, xxxii, 9, 29, 32, 33, 38, 40, 42, 43, 50, 96, 105, 107, 116, 123, 136, 149, 153, 154, 158, 161, 180
   and possiblity of Ashenbach as manager, xxiv–xxv, xxix
Clapp, John, 86
Clark, Bob, 107
Clark, William H. (Dad), 125
Clarke, Fred, 171
Clarke, Joe, xxiv(fn)
Clarksburg, West Virginia, 22, 205
Clarksville, Tennessee, 23, 212
Class A baseball, 17, 18
Class B baseball, 18, 19, 88
Class C baseball, 19, 20
Class D baseball, 20–24
Clay, Billy, 77

INDEX

Clay Center, Kansas, 20
Cleburne, Texas, 208
Cleveland Spiders, xv
Cleveland, Ohio, 35
Cleveland (American League club), xv, 31, 35, 38, 39, 107, 117, 181
Clingman, Billy, 107
Clinton, Iowa, 23
Clymer, Otis, 31
Clymer, William J., 99–101, *173*
Coalinga, California, 22, 206
Cobb, Ty, 39
Cockhill, 31, 33
Collins, Jimmie, 54, 85
Columbia, South Carolina, 19, 58, 60, 68, 197
Columbus, Georgia, 19, 197
Columbus, Nebraska, 24, 200
Columbus, Ohio, 17, 99, 117, 182
Comiskey, Charles, 128
Connecticut League, 13, 18, 23, 87, 88, 191
Connellsville, Pennsylvania, 23
Conners, Tom (umpire), 104
Connery, Tom, 81, 82
Cooney, 30
Corbett, James J. (boxer), 133
Corcoran, Mickey, 154
Corcoran, Tom, 153
Corpus Christi, Texas, 22, 201
Corsicana, Texas, 208

Cortland, New York, 158
Costello, 35
Cotton States League, 20, 211
Coughlin, Bill, xxvii, 31, 157
Coveleskie, Harry, 103-106
Crab, The (surly player behavior), 137–139
Craig, Lefty, 90, 91
Creamer, Theodore B., 28
Cree, Birdie, 31, 102
Criger, Lou, 85
Crist, Chester, 31, 108
Crockoe, 109, 110
Crooks, Jack, 32
Crowder, A.C., 20
Cunningham, E.H., 131–133
Curtis, Cliff, 156
Cusack, Steve (umpire), 80

Dallas Defenders, xvii(fn)
Dallas Steers, xvi–xvii
Dallas, Texas, 8, 20, 49, 93, 126, 133, 153
Daniels, Bert, 31
Danville, Illinois, 19, 187
Danville, Virginia, 19, 187
Davenport, Iowa, 19, 187
Davis, J. Ira "Slats," 127, 128
Dayton, Ohio, xxvii, 18, 124, 142, 186
Decatur, Illinois, 23
Decker, Al, 108
Deininger, Otto, 30, 32
Deisel, Henry, 108
Deisel, Jack, 108
Delehanty, Joe, 31

HUMOR AMONG THE MINORS

Dennison, Texas, 208
Denver, Colorado, 17, 185
Depew, Chauncey M., 12
Des Moines, Iowa, 17, 116, 185
Detroit (American League club), xxiv, xxvii, xxviii, 31, 33, 38, 39, 61, 157–159, *160*, 170, 181
Devereaux, William "Brick," xx(fn)
Devlin, Arthur, 10, 42
Dexter, Charles, 108
Dickerson, E. W., 22
Dickinson, B. S., 22
Doescher, 30, 32
Donahue, Red, 35
Donahue, John "Jiggs," 124, 125
Donovan, Bill "Duffy," 61–63
Donovan, Pat, 171
Dooin, Charles "Red," 107, 111, 171
Doughtery, Pat, 29, 31
Dowd, Tommy, 54, 55
Dowdell, 91
Doyle, Jack, 157
Drake, Delos, 31, 143
Drury, Bob, 89
Dubuque, Iowa, 19, 187
Duluth, Minnesota, 20
Dunn, D. P., 23
Dunn, Jack, 143, 157
Durham, Louis "Bull," 30
Durrett, Ike, 43

Eagan, Bad Bill, 161
Earle, Howard J., 70–72
East Liverpool, Ohio, 19, 195

Eastern Carolina League, 210
Eastern Kansas League, 22, 202
Eastern League, 13, 17, 29, 50, 65, 78, 154, 183
Eau Claire, Wisconsin, 20
Eckstrom, C. J., 19
Edmonton, Alberta, 19, 198
Egan Dick, 30
Egan, Wish, 100
El Paso, Texas, 194
El Reno, Oklahoma, 19
Elberfield, Norman "Kid," 107
Elgin, Illinois, 23
Elkhart, Indiana, 23, 207
Elliot, J. A., 20
Ellsworth, Kansas, 20
Elmira, New York, 18, 189
Elwert, Bill, 108
Ely, Frederick "Bones," 117
Engel, George, 155
Enid, Oklahoma, 19, 194
Erie, Pennsylvania, 19, 195
Evansville (Indiana) River Rats, xxii
Evansville, Indiana, 18, 186
Ewing, William "Buck," 63, 106, 108

Factoryville, Pennsylvania, 157
Fairmont, West Virginia, 22, 23, 205
Fairview Park (Dayton, Ohio), 142

INDEX

Falkenberg, Frederick "Cy," 31
Fall River, Massachusetts, 18, 190
Fans
   advice from Ed Ashenback, 174, 175
   as a mob, 45, 46, 47
   on the field, 45
   of German nationality, 156, 157
Farnsworth, William C., 28
Farnsworth Cup, 28
Farrell, John H., 13–15, 17, 18, *48*
Farrell, Jack, 31, 32, 107
Fayetteville, North Carolina, 21, 210
Field of Dreams, xxii
Fielding, xv(fn)
Finn, Mickey, 150, 151
Finn, Mike J., 120, 121
Fisher, E. B., 22
Fitzsimmons, Bob (boxer), 133
Flanagan, James "Steamer," 158
Flanner, Joseph, 14
Flater, Jack, 70, 71, 102
Flint, Michigan, 21, 218
Flood, Tim, 32, 79
Fond du Lac, Wisconsin, 21, 199
Forbes Field (Pittsburgh, Pennsylvania), 146
Foreman, Frank, 100
Fort Wayne, Indiana, 18, 142
Fort Worth Colts, xvii, xvii(fn)
Fort Worth Panthers, xvi
Fort Worth, Texas, xvi(fn), 20
Foster, Ed, 31, 101, 102, 104
Frankfort, Kentucky, 20, 214
Freedman, Andrew, 9
Freeman, John "Buck," 31, 158
Freeport, Illinois, 21, 23
Fremont, Nebraska, 24, 200
Fresco, California, 24
Fruitvale, California, 24
Fuller, William "Shorty," 106

Gadsden, Alabama, 22, 204
Galesburg, Illinois, 21, 216
Galveston, Texas, 20, 147
Gary, Indiana, 23, 207
Geier, Phil, 79, 80
George, Lefty, 32
Geyer, Lefty, 108, 142, 143
Gibson, Norwood, 85
Gilbert, Billy, 30
Gilks, Bob, 107, 120
Gilligan, Reddy, 164, 165
Gloversville, Pennsylvania, 63
Godar, Johnnie, 107
Golden, Roy, 107
Goldsboro, North Carolina, 21, 210
Goode, 144
Goshen, Indiana, 23, 207
Gosnell, C. A., 23
Grady, Mike, 30
Graffius, William J., xvii

— 227

Grafton, West Virginia, 22, 23, 205
Graham, 51, 145, 146
Graham, Archibald "Moonlight," xxi–xxii
Graham, George M., *80*, 114, 115
Graham, Thomas F., 17
Grand Island, Nebraska, 24
Grand Rapids, Michigan, 18, 22, 134, 186
Grant, John D., xxvi
Gray, Thomas, 34
Great Bend, Kansas, 20
Green Bay, Wisconsin, 21, 199
Greensboro, North Carolina, 22, 209
Greenville, South Carolina, 22, 209
Greenwood, Mississippi, 20, 211
Gresham, Claude, xxiv(fn)
Griffin, Sandy, 98, 112
Griffith, Clark, xxxiii, 171
Grim, John J., 67, 68, 108
Grim, Jack, 58, 60, 154
Gronninger, J. D., 23
Groundskeepers, 119–121
Guthrie, Oklahoma, 19, 194

Halderman, C. W., 20
Hamilton, Billy, 29, 30
Hampton Crabs, xviii
Hampton, Virginia, 9, 40, 41, 131, 132, 164, 165
Hanlon, Ned, 66, 166
Hannibal, Missouri, 21, 216
Harrisburg Ponies, xv

Harrisburg, Pennsylvania, 18, 28, 29, 34, 58, 102, 192
Hart, William F. "Billy," 108, 115-118
Hartford, Connecticut, 18, 78, 81, 191
Hartley (Walter "Chick"?), 31
Hastings, Nebraska, 21, 200
Hattiesburg, Mississippi, 20, 211
Hauser, Ben, 31
Haverhill, Massachusetts, 18, 57, 190
Hayden, Jack, 30
Haymond, T. S., 22
Heckert, George, 29, 90, 91
Hedges, Robert, 110
Helmund, George, 108
Henderson, Kentucky, 23, 212
Henke, Louis, 111, 112
Henn, Jack, 108
Hennessey, Joe, 102, 108
Herman, Frank, 24
Herrmann, August, *12*, 171
Herrmann, Garry, 110
Herzog, Charles "Buck," 30
Hiawatha, Kansas, 22
Hinchman, Bill, 31
Hoban (Rev. Archbishop), 83
Hoban, Walter C., *80*, 114, 115
Hoch, Harry, 31
Hoey, Jack, 31
Hoffman, 31

INDEX

Hogriever, George, 6, 108
Holland, Michigan, 22, 217
Holly, Eddie, 30, 32
Holmes, Jim, 30
Holton, Kansas, 22, 202
Holyoke, Massachusetts, 18, 135, 191
Hoquiam, Washington, 22
Hopkinsville, Kentucky, 20, 23, 212
Horse races,
   players going to, 158–160
Horton, Kansas, 22, 202
Hostutler, P. H., 20
Hot Springs, Arkansas, xvii, 158
Houselman, Jimmy, 108
Houston Buffaloes, xvii
Houston, Texas, 20, 126
Huggins, Miller, 107
Hughey, James H., 117
Hulseman, 31
Humor Among the Minors, xxiii, xxx–xxxii
   Ashenbach's nervous breakdown attributed to, xxix
Huntington, Indiana, 21, 203
Huntington, West Virginia, 23, 213
Hutchinson, Kansas, 20

Indiana-Michigan League, 207
Indianapolis, Indiana, 17, 90, 91, 117, 182
Inter-State League, xvii, 8, 76, 142

Jacklitsch, Fred, 30
Jackson, Jimmie, 31
Jackson, Michigan, 218
Jackson, Mississippi, 20, 211
Jacksonville, Florida, 19, 52, 53, 58, 197
Jacksonville, Illinois, 21, 23
Jennings, Hughey, xix, xxiv, xxviii, 136, *160*, 169–171
Jersey City, New Jersey, 17, 183
Johnson, Al, 35
Johnson, Ban, 110, 171
Johnson, Jack (boxer), 177
Johnson City, Tennessee, 22, 204
Johnstown Johnnies, xxv
Johnstown, Pennsylvania, xxv(fn), 11, 18, 29, 34, 63, 65, 66, 103, 104, 124, 149, 192
Joliet, Illinois, 23
Jones, Tom, 31
Jonesboro, Arkansas, 21
Jordan, Tim, 54, 55
Joyce, Mike, 143
Joyner, W.R., 19
Jude, Frank, 144
Junction City, Kansas, 20
Justice, M. E., 21

Kahoe, Mike, 107
Kalamazoo, Michigan, 21, 218
Kankakee, Illinois, 23, 212
Kansas City, Missouri, 17, 79, 80, 180, 182

Kansas City Mouse, 134
Kansas League, 20, 108
Kavanaugh, Judge W. M., 13, 14, 17
Kearney, Nebraska, 23, 200
Keister, Billy, 30
Kelly, George "King," 53, 122, 123
Kelly, Joe, 153, 166
Kelly, Mike, 35, 36, 173
Kelly, Shamokin Mop-Up, 152, 153
Kentucky-Illinois-Tennessee League, 23, 212
Keokuk, Iowa, 21, 216
Kerwin, Dan, 153
Kewanee, Illinois, 21
Killifer, Red, 31
Kilroy, 35
Kline, George K., 34
Kling, 63
Klusman, Billy, 107
Knoxville, Tennessee, 22, 204
Kohnle, William, 108
Kokomo, Indiana, 21, 203
Kolb, Eddie, 108
Konnick, Mike, 158
Kraemer, J. H., 20
Krause, Ed, 31
Krehmeier, Charles, 126
Kroh, Floyd "Rube," xxix(fn), 30

La Crosse, Wisconsin, 20
Lachance, George "Candy," 85
Lafayette, Indiana, 21, 203
Lajoie, Napoleon, 79, 171

Lake, Fred, 55, 171
Lally, Bud (umpire), 137
Lancaster, Ohio, 21, 215
Lancaster, Pennsylvania, 19, 103, 156, 192
Lansing, Michigan, 21, 218
Laredo, Textas, 22, 201
Larkin, Ted, 35
Larned, Kansas, 20
LaRoy, Lewis, 31, 144, 145, 156
Latham, Arlie, xix
Lauterborn, Billy, 32
Lawrence, Massachusetts, 18, 171, 190
Lebanon, Pennsylvania, 28
Lehighton, Pennsylvania, 170
Lelivelt, 31
Lennon, George, xxvii
Lennox, Eddie, 30, 32
Lethbridge, Alberta, 19, 198
Lewis, Fred, 30
Lexington, Kentucky, 20, 214
Lima, Ohio, 21, 215
Lincoln, Nebraska, 17, 116, 144, 185
Lincoln Park (Cincinnati), 115
Lindsay, R. H., 18
Lister, Pete, 31, 101
Little Rock, Arkansas, 117, 120, 121, 152
Lobert, Hans, 29, 30
Loftus, Tom, 7, 37
London, England, 87
Long Beach, California, 23

INDEX

Longview Hospital (Cincinnati), xxxiii, xxxiv
Los Angeles Giants, xviii
Los Angeles, California, 17, 23, 127, 188
Louisville, Kentucky, 17, 99, 100, 108, 157, 182
Lowell, Massachusetts, 18, 55, 171, 190
Lucas, W. H., 13, 14
Lucid, Cornelius "Con," 78
Lush, Johnnie, 31, 33
Lynch, Mike, 31
Lynch, Thomas J., 171
Lynchburg, Virginia, 19, 40, 131, 196
Lynn, Massachusetts, 18, 190
Lyons, Denny, 106
Lyons, Kansas, 20
Lytle, Edward "Pop," 76, 77

M. A. Donahue & Co., xxxi
Mack, Joseph "Reddy," 108
Macomb, Illinois, 21
Mack, Connie, 50, 68-70, 122, 144, 167-169, 171
Macon Brigands, xxii(fn)
Macon Highlanders, xxiii
Macon, Georgia, 19, 46, 47, 49, 58, 84, 108, 197
   Ashenbach spikes a boy in, xxiii–xxiv
Madison, Wisconsin, 21, 199
Madisonville, Kentucky, 23, 212
Maiers, The, 23

Major league players, 160, 161
Malay, Charles, 30
Manchester, New Hampshire, xxii, 55
Manhattan, Kansas, 20
Manhattans club (Cincinnati), xiv, 6
Manning, Walter "Rube," 31
Mannington, West Virginia, 22, 205
Mansfield Haymakers, 76, 77
Mansfield, Ohio, 19, 21, 76, 195
Marianna, Arkansas, 21
Marion, Indiana, 20, 21, 203
Marion, Ohio, 21, 215
Marr, Charles "Lefty," 107, 111, 112
Marriage, at home plate, 119, 120
Martell, (Leon?), 30
Marysville, Kansas, 24, 203
Matthews, Harry, 108
Matthews, William, 31
Mathewson, Christy, xviii–xix, 9, 40, 132, 133, 156, 157, 166
Mattern, Al, 30
Maysville, Kentucky, 20, 214
McAleer, James, 171
McBride, Ralph, 123, 124
McCabe, James "Swat," 158
McCarthy, Jack, 96
McCloskey, John, 143
McCloskey, John J., 155

McCormick, J. P., 23
McCormick, Jerry, 35
McCormicks, The, 23
McCullom, William, 56
McDiarmid, Campbell J., 110
McElveen, Pryor "Humpty," 30
McFarlane, W. R., 22
McGee, Lee, 107
McGilvray, Bill, 30
McGinnity, Joe, 166
McGlynn, Ulysses "Stoney," 31
McGowan, 73, 74
McGraw, John, 94, 95, 103, 105, *128*, 145, 160, 165–167, 171
McGrew, 108
McGuire (groundskeeper), 62, 63
McKeesport, Pennsylvania, 19, 195
McKernan, Ed, 96, 108
McLean, John, 54, 55
McLean, Larry, 57, 118
McPherson, Kansas, 20
Medicine Hat, Alberta, 19, 198
Memphis, Tennessee, 18, 96, 184
Meyers, John "Chief," 30, 144
Michigan State League, 22, 108, 217
Middletown, Connecticut, 23, 86
Millcreek Bottoms club, xiv, 6, 108
Miller, George F. "Doggie," 142, 143
Miller, Warren, 52

Millerick, Patrick, 150
Milligan, Big Jack, 35
Milwaukee, Wisconsin, 17, 21, 117, 156, 157, 182
Minneapolis, Minnesota, 17, 20, 69, 117, 182
Minnesota-Wisconsin League, 20
Minooka, Pennsylvania, 64, 83
Minor league players,
    and contract of, 24–28
    and fans, 126–128
    and fatalities, 111, 112
    and money from fans, 41, 42
    and road trips, 55
    and salaries, 164, 165
    and superstitions, 143, 144
Missouri-Iowa-Nebraska-Kansas League, 24
Mobile, Alabama, 18, 184
Moll, Charles F., 21
Monmouth, Illinois, 21, 216
Montaseno, Washington, 22
Montgomery, Alabama, 184
Montgomery, West Virginia, 23, 213
Montreal, Quebec, 17, 183
Moonlight, Arthur (fictitious), 25, 28
Moose Jaw, Saskatchewan, 19, 198
Moran, John "Herbie," 30
Moreland, G. L., 19
Morgantown, West Virginia, 23

INDEX

Morristown, Tennessee, 22, 204
Morse, Whitey, 108
Mosquito Valley League (fictitious), 141
Mowrey, Mike, 31
Mulford, Red, Jr., xiii, xiv, xiv(fn), xxvi, xxvii, xxvi(fn), xxxiv, 6, 35, 38
Mullen, Jimmie, 158
Mulvey, Joe, 35
Murnane, Tim H., 13, 14, 18, 55, 58, 86, 152
Murphy (groundskeeper), 120, 121
Murphy, Charles W., xxix(fn), 40, 110
Murray, Ernie, 50, 51
Muscatine, Iowa, 23
Muskegon, Michigan, 22, 217
Mustaches, on players, 135, 136
Muskogee, Oklahoma, 19, 194
Myers, John H., 34
Myers, Lolla, 108

Napa, California, 24
Nashua, New Hampshire, xxii, 10, 53
Nashville, Tennessee, 18, 62, 63, 108, 184
  ballpark in, 148
National Association of Minor Leagues, 14–16, 34
National Association of Professional Baseball Clubs, 25, 80, 88, 168
National Board (minor leagues), 13-15, 88
National Commission (major leagues), xxvi, *16*, 110, 165, 171
National League, xxix, 13, 15, 16, 29, 34, 36, 54, 70, 81, 87, 100, 106, 113, 115, 132, 159
Naugatuck Valley League, 87
Nebraska City, Nebraska, 24
Nebraska State League, 24, 200
National Commission, xxiii
Needham, Tom, 30, 32
Nemec, Ray, xv(fn)
Ness, Jack, 31
New Bedford, Massachusetts, 18, 190
New Britain, Connecticut, 18, 191
New Castle Quakers, xvii
New Castle, Pennsylvania, 8, 19, 76, 108, 136, 137, 195
New England League, xxii, 10, 13, 18, 53, 56, 190
New Haven, Connecticut, 18, 191
New London, Connecticut, 23
New Orleans, Louisiana, 18, 108, 152, 184
  ballpark in, 147
New York (American League club), 29, 31, 102, 108, 181

— 233

New York (National
  League club), xix, 10,
  30, 42, 86, 87, 105–107,
  125, *128*, 132, 133, 144,
  145, 158, 160, 165–167
New York City, New York,
  9, 17, 104, 113, 125,
  132, 165
New York State League,
  xviii, xxii, xxiv, xxv,
  xxvii, xxix, 11, 18, 51,
  56, 63, 64, 70, 72, 88,
  97, 99, 108, 114, 158,
  180, 189
New York World, 73
Newark, New Jersey, 17,
  183
Newark, Ohio, 21, 158,
  215
Newport News-Hampton
  Shipbuilders, xix–xx
Newport News, Virginia,
  10, 40, 41, 121, 132
Newton, Kansas, 20
Niles, Michigan, 23, 207
Noonan, Pete, 153
Norfolk Phenoms, xviii,
  xviii(fn)
Norfolk, Virginia, 9, 40,
  131–133, 196
North Carolina League,
  xviii(fn), xxi, xxii(fn), 10,
  42, *96*, 122
Northampton,
  Massachusetts, 18, 191
Northeast Arkansas
  League, 21
Northern Association, 23
Northern State League of
  Indiana, 20, 203
Northwestern League, 13,
  18, 193

Norwich, Connecticut, 23

O'Conner, Mike, 133, 134
O'Hara, Tom, 102
O'Loughlin, Francis
  "Silk," 113
O'Neil, Jack, 157, 158
O'Neil, Mike, 31, 157
O'Neil, N.L., 17
O'Rourke (policeman), 47
O'Rourke, James H., 13,
  14, 18, *64*, 86–88, 115
O'Rourke, Tim (umpire),
  136, 137
Oakland, California, 21,
  188
Ohio-Michigan League, xv
Ohio-Pennsylvania
  League, 19, 108, 195
Ohio State League, 21, 37,
  215
Oklahoma City,
  Oklahoma, 20
Omaha, Nebraska, 17, 185
Oshkosh, Wisconsin, 21,
  199
Osteen, James "Champ,"
  50
Oswego, New York, 147,
  148
Ottumwa, Iowa, 21, 216
Outlaw leagues, 28–30,
  32

Pacific Coast League, 17,
  188
Padden, Dick, xxvii
Paducah, Kentucky, 23,
  212
Palestine, Texas, 208
Palmer, 121
Paragould, Arkansas, 21

INDEX

Paris, Kentucky, 20, 96, 108, 214
Paris, Texas, 208
Parkersburg, West Virginia, 23, 213
Pasadena, California, 23
Paterson (New Jersey) Silk Weavers, xvi
Pattee, Harry, 30
Pauxtis, Simon "Si," 30
Pearson, Alec, 33
Pekin, Illinois, 21
Pennsylvania State League, xv, xvi, 8, 35, 37
Pennsylvania and West Virginia League, 23
Peoria, Illinois, 19, 117, 187
Perrine, Colonel, 34
Perry, 77, 78
Persons, Eddie, 50, 57
Petaluma, California, 24
Petersburg, Virginia, 40, 132
Pfeister, Jack, 107
Philadelphia (American League club), 31, 70, 87, 102, 106, 107, 116, 144, 167, 181
Philadelphia (National League club), 30, 31, 104, 105, 107, 108, 111, 180
Philadelphia North American, 80, 114, 115
Philadelphia, Pennsylvania, 28, 32, 80, 91, 146, 161, 166
Pittsburgh (National League club), 30, 33, 43, 70, 107, 180
Pittsburgh, Pennsylvania, 19, 65, 117, 134, 146, 161
Phyle, Bill, 30
Plank, Eddie, 103, 169
Point, The (Johnstown, Pennsylvania ballpark), 124
Point Pleasant, West Virginia, 23, 213
Point Richmond, California, 24
Polo Grounds (New York ballpark), 103, 104
Portland, Maine, 54
Portland, Oregon, 17, 154, 155, 188, 193
Portsmouth, Ohio, 21, 215
Portsmouth, Virginia, xx, 19, 40, 196
Pottsville, Pennsylvania, 83, 148
Powell, Abner, 123
Powers, P. T., 13, 14
Proctor, R. E., 23
Providence Grays, 87
Providence, Rhode Island, 17, 183
Puttman, Ambrose, 108

Quincy, Illinois, 21, 216
Quinn (umpire), xxi(fn)

Racine, Wisconsin, 21, 199
Raleigh, North Carolina, xix, 21, 122, 210
Ramsey, Hank, 88, 89, 158
Ramsey, Tom "Toad," 116
Ransick, Edward, 108

Rath, Morris, 31
Raymer, Fred, 32
Raymond, E. H., 24
Raymond, Washington, 22
Read, R. W., 21
Reading, Pennsylvania, xvi, 19, 156, 192
Red Cloud, Nebraska, 24, 200
Red Wing, Minnesota, 20
Redondo, California, 23
Reeder, Ed, 107
Regina, Saskatchewan, 19, 198
Reilly, John, 107
Reilly, Joseph "Josh," xxxii, 74, 75
Reisling, Dr., 31
Rhodes, Charlie "Dusty," 31
Richmond, Kentucky, 20, 214
Richmond, Virginia, xix, 19, 40, 42, 132, 196
Rickert, Joe, 76, 77
Roach, Wilbur "Roxey," 31
Roanoke, Virginia, 19, 40, 131, 196
Rochester, Minnesota, 20
Rochester, New York, 17, 183
Rock Island, Illinois, 19, 187
Rockfort, Illinois, 21, 199
Rocky Mount, North Carolina, 21, 210
Rohe, George, 107
Rome, Georgia, 22, 204
Rome, New York, 146
Roosevelt, Theodore, 169
Roth, Frank, 156
Rusie, Amos, 133

Ryan, Ray, 108
Ryder, Jack, xxx, xxxi, 12

Sabetha, Texas, 202
Sacramento Senators, xx–xxi, xx(fn)
Sacramento, California, 17, 188
Saginaw, Michigan, 21, 218
Sales, Eddie, 35
Salina, Kansas, 20
Sallee, Harry "Slim," 30
San Antonio, Texas, 20, 93, 94
San Francisco, California, 17, 23, 75, 128, 147, 188
San Joaquin Valley League, 22, 206
San Jose, California, 23
San Leandre, California, 24
San Rafael, California, 24
Santa Ana, California, 23
Santa Clara College, 171
Sapulpa, Oklahoma, 19, 194
Sarsaparilla club (or league) (fictitious), 25, 137, 141
Savannah, Georgia, 19, 47, 58, *176*, 197
Schaefer, Charley, 80, 81, 158, 159, *176*
Schlei, George, 107
Schmelz, Gustavus "Gus," 161
Schmit, Frederick "Crazy," 94
Schnectady Electricians, xviii

INDEX

Schnectady, New York, xxiv, xxvii
Schrall, Joe, 108, 112, 113, 134
Schweitzer, Al "Cheese," 107
Scranton Miners, xxv-xxvi, xxvi(fn), xxviii
Scranton, Pennsylvania, 11, 18, 33, 35, 51, 63-65, 73, 83, 89, 114, 135, 145-147, 157, 170, 189
Seattle, Washington, 18, 193
Sebring, Jimmy, 10, 30, 33, 42, 43
Seneca, Kansas, 22, 202
Seventh Ward Fishing Club (Cincinnati), xxvii(fn)
Seward, Nebraska, 24, 200
Sexton, M.H., 14, 15, *32*
Seymour, James "Cy," 158, 160
Shaffer, Charley, 84-86
Shamokin, Pennsylvania, 83
Sharpe, Bayard "Bud," 30
Sharpe, Peck, 142
Shaw, Royal "Hunky," 30
Shaw, J. H., 19
Shea, Dennis, 154, 155
Shea, John "Nap," 112, 113
Shean, Dave, 30, 101
Sheboygan, Wisconsin, 144, 145
Shenandoah, Iowa, 24
Shenandoah, Pennsylvania, xvi
Sherman, Texas, 208
Shettler, 30
Shibe Park (Philadelphia ballpark), 146
Shortell, Ed, 97, 98
Shreveport Giants, xxii
Shreveport, Louisiana, 10, 20, 43, 62, 73, 120, 150-152
Sievers, H. A., 24
Sioux City, Iowa, 116, 117, 185
Sipps, George (pseudonym), 28
Smink, Bill, 78, 79
Smith, Frank, 122, 123
Smith, Fred, 30
Smith, Sidney, 39, 50, 51, 68
Smith, William A. "Billy," 47, 58
Sockalexis, Louis, 144
South Atlantic League, xxii, 10, 12, 19, 38, 58, 59, 68, 108, 197
South Bend, Indiana, 18, 186
South Michigan League, 218
Southeastern League, 22, 204
Southern California Trolley League, 23
Southern League, xv, xix, xxi, xxii, 8, 10, 13, 17, 43, 49, 93, 105, 108, 115, 117, 120, 149, 150, 152, 184
Southern Michigan Association, 21
Southwest Texas Baseball League, 22

Southwestern League, 201

Spartanburg, South Carolina, 22, 209

Spokane, Washington, 18, 81, 154, 155, 193

Sporting Life, xv, xvi, xxi, xxiv, xxvii, xxx

Sporting News, The, 14

Springfield (Ohio) Governors, xvii, xxxi

Springfield, Illinois, 19, 187

Springfield, Massachusetts, 18, 191

Springfield, Missouri, 19, 194

Springfield, Ohio, 8, 74, 186

St. Johns, New Brunswick, 54

St. Joseph, Missouri, 17, 80, 86, 185

St. Louis (American Association club), 107

St. Louis (American League club), 110, 159, 181

St. Louis (National League club), 31, 33, 50, 107, 117, 155, 180

St. Louis, Missouri, 14, 126

St. Mary Cemetery (Cincinnati), xxxiv

St. Paul Saints, xxvi, xxviii

St. Paul, Minnesota, xxiii, xxv, 11, 17, 68, 69, 79, 80, 127, 144, 148, 149, 156, 157, 159, 160, 182

Stahl, Charles "Chick," 85

Stallings, George, 65

Stanton (umpire), 43

Starnagle, George, 30, 32

Starr, Charles, 30

Steele, Bill, 30

Stem, Fred, 30

Stenzel, Jack, 106

Stockton, California, 23

Stratford (Connecticut) Ocedas, 86

Straus, Joe, 107

Street, Charley, 31

Strouthers, Con, 43, 58, 60

Sugen, Joe, 156

Suggs, George, 42, 54, 55

Sullivan, Billy, 63

Sullivan, Sutor, 100, 101

Sullivan, Ted, xvi, 8. 49, 92-94, 96, 126, 133

Sunday baseball, 82–84, 145, 146

Superior, Nebraska, 24, 200

Superior, Wisconsin, 20

Susquehanna League, 56

Sutthoff, Jack, 107

Swacina, Harry, 30

Swamp Root ball club (fictitious), 141

Sweeney, 35

Sweeney, Bill, 107

Swift, Marty, 35

Syracuse Stars, xxix–xxx, xxxii

Syracuse, New York, 11, 18, 32, 63, 97, 98, 108, 112, 144, 146, 189

Tacoma, Washington, 18, 22, 193

Taft, C. P., 111

INDEX

Tannehill, Jesse, 85, 107
Tannehill, Lee, 42, 107
Tarboro, North Carolina, xx, 147
Taylor, John, 84–86
Taylor, Texas, 208
Tearney, A. R., 19
Tebeau, Pat, 7
Terre Haute, Indiana, 18, 186
Texas Association, xvii, xvii(fn), 208
Texas League, 20, 108
Texas-Southern League, xvi
Thielman, Jake, 155
Thoney, Jack, 107
Three-I League, 19, 168, 187
Tiemeyer, Ed, 108
Tighe, Jack, 81, 96, 168, 169
Toledo, Ohio, 17, 108, 151, 171, 182
Toman, Jimmy, xvi
Topeka, Kansas, 17, 185
Toronto, Ontario, 17, 183
Torreyson, Frank, 134
Townsend, Jack, 102
Traverse City, Michigan, 22, 217
Trenton, New Jersey, 19, 34, 90, 192
Tri-State League, xiv, xiv(fn), xxviii, xxviii(fn), xxix, 6, 11, 28, 34, 52, 65, 66, 77, 90, 97, 101, 103, 104, *112*, 114, 115, 124, 149, 168, 192
  Ashenbach's opinion on salary limit, xxvi
Trout, C., 34

Troy, New York, 18, 146, 147, 189
Truxton, New York, 171
Tulare, California, 22 208
Tunis, Bill, 34

Umpires, 43, 56–58, 68, 69, 71, 72, 78, 80, 84, 95, 104, 127, 128, 136, 137, 142, 143, 152, 153, 156, 173, 175
Unglaub, Bob, 31, 33
Union League, 115
Uniontown, Pennsylvania, 23
University of North Carolina, xxi
University of South Carolina, xxi(fn)
Upp, George, 30
Urbana, Ohio, 115
Ussery, Dr. W. C., 20
Utica, New York, 189, 63, 70, 72, 189

Valdois, Fred "Red," 108
Vallejo, California, 24
Vancouver, British Columbia, 18, 193
Vaughn, Harry, 107, 149, 150
Veil, Frederick "Bucky," 30
Vernon, California, 188
Vickers, Harry "Rube," 31
Vicksburg, Mississippi, 20, 211
Victoria, British Columbia, 193
Victoria, Texas, 22, 201

Vincennes, Indiana, 23, 212
Vinson, Ernest "Rube," 31
Virginia League, xviii, 9, 12, 19, 40, 42, 67, 108, 122, 131–133
Virginia-North Carolina League, xviii, 10, 12
Virginia Valley League, 23, 213
Visalia, California, 22, 206
Voss, Alex, 107

Wabash, Indiana, 21, 203
Waco, Texas, 20
Waddell, Rube, 103, 122
Walker, Tom (umpire), 58
Ward, Frank "Piggy," 157
Ward, John M., 133
Warhop, Jack, 31, 102
Washington (American League club), xxxiii, 29, 31, 33, 87, 107, 181
Washington, D.C., 84, 122
Washington State League, 22
Waterbury, Connecticut, 191
Waterloo, Iowa, 19, 21, 187
Watkins, 90
Wausau, Wisconsin, 20
Wearn, J. H., 22
Weddige, Al, 41, 42
Weidner, Bill, 107
Wellington, Kansas, 20
Werden, Percy (umpire), 69, 156
Werrick, Joe, 76, 77
West Side Park (Chicago), 129

West Virginia League, 22, 108, 205
Western Association, 19, 194
Western Canada League, 19, 198
Western League, 17, 80, 86, 108, 116, 117, 144, 185
Whalen, (William?), 31
Wheeling, West Virginia, 18, 186
Whitaker, Dr. Joel, 21
Whitney, E. M., 22
Wiggs, Jim, 30, 32
Wilkes-Barre Barons, xxx
Wilkes Barre, Pennsylvania, 18, 33, 56, 63-65, 83, 99, 100, 114, 143, 147, 153, 157, 189
Wilmington (North Carolina) Sailors, xxii
Wilmington, Delaware, 28, 34, 192
Wilmington, North Carolina, xx, 21, 44, 46, 210
Williams, C. R., 19
Williamsport, Pennsylvania, xxv, 19, 28, 29, 33, 34, 101, 102
Willimantic, Connecticut, 23
Wilmot, Walter, 84
Wilson, North Carolina, 21, 210
Wiltse, George "Hooks," 30
Winchester, Kentucky, 20, 214
Winnepeg, Manitoba, 19, 198

INDEX

Winona, Minnesota, 20
Winston-Salem, North
  Carolina, 22, 209
Wisconsin-Illinois League,
  21, 199
Wisconsin State League,
  108
Wise, Sam, 35
Wiseman, Julius "Doc,"
  108, 148
Witchita, Kansas, 17, 185
Wolter, Harry, 31
Wolters, Jack, 36
Wolverton, Harry, 30, 52,
  101, 102
Wood, George, 35
Woodruff, Orville, 107
Woonsocket, Rhode
  Island, 171
Worchester,
  Massachusetts, 18, 190
Wright, George, 87
Wright, Harry, 87

Yale University, 88
Yancey, Hogan, 50, 51
Yazoo City, Mississippi,
  20, 211
Yeagar, George, 108
York, Pennsylvania, 19,
  28, 29, 192
Young, Denton "Cy," xiv–
  xv, xiv(fn), xv(fn), xviii,
  7, 9, 38, 85, 115
Young, J. N., 22
Youngstown, Ohio, 19,
  108, 171, 195

Zanesville, Ohio, 18
"Zeekoe," xxxi–xxxii, 75

Titles available from

BRAYBREE
Publishing

The Jackson Generals: Minor League Baseball in Jackson, Tennessee
by Kevin D. McCann • ISBN 978-0-9671251-7-6

History of the Detection, Conviction, Life and Designs of John A. Murrell, the Great Western Land Pirate
by Augustus Q. Walton, Esq. • ISBN 978-1-940127-02-6

A Sacred High Place: A History of Mount Carmel Cemetery and Meetinghouse, McNairy County, Tennessee
by John E. Talbott, J.D. • ISBN 978-0-9671251-9-0

A History of Dickson County, Tennessee
by Dr. Robert E. Corlew • ISBN 978-1-940127-00-2

Gold is the Key: Murder, Robbery, & the Gold Rush in Jackson, Tennessee
by Thomas L. Aud • ISBN 978-0-9671251-3-8

The Peg Leg Politician: Adam Huntsman of Tennessee
by Kevin D. McCann • ISBN 978-0-9671251-4-5

Hurst's Wurst: Colonel Fielding Hurst & the Sixth Tennessee Cavalry U.S.A.
by Kevin D. McCann • ISBN 978-0-9671251-2-1